HOW TO START A SUCCESSFUL FOOD TRUCK BUSINESS

QUIT YOUR DAY JOB AND EARN FULL-TIME
INCOME ON AUTOPILOT WITH A PROFITABLE
FOOD TRUCK BUSINESS EVEN IF YOU'RE AN
ABSOLUTE BEGINNER

WALTER GRANT

ANDREW HUDSON

Thank you for your choosing this book.
If you enjoy this book or find it to be helpful, please consider leaving a review
on Amazon.

To go directly to the review page, you can:

- Scan the QR-code below with the camera on your phone
- Or type in the Shorturl link above the QR-code in your internet
  browser

shorturl.at/HMEIK

CONTENTS

INTRODUCTION

Whatever you can do, or dream you can, begin it.
Boldness has genius, power, and magic in it.
— Johann Wolfgang von Goethe

Are food trucks a foodie's dream come true or just a fad? Okay, we will admit that there is a lot of hype around food trucks right now, but we predict that this hype is here to stay. In fact, what other food business trend have you seen that has managed to establish its own industry and earn a market value of $1.2 billion (IbisWorld, 2021)?

Think of the very first place you saw a food truck (and no… hotdog stands don't count here). It was probably at a food market, festival, or local park. From the beginning, food truck businesses positioned themselves differently from typical restaurants. Yes, they served food like any other fast food joint, but each truck operated in carefully marked locations and catered to its own specific target audience.

The food truck owners were clear with their message: We are not for everyone!

That type of message wouldn't fly for your traditional restaurant which sets up shop in central locations, creates menus to cater to a diverse audience, and satisfies many people with very different food preferences. For instance, nowadays, it's common to find restaurants catering to meat lovers, vegans, as well as those who are downright picky eaters!

Food truck businesses offer the creative foodpreneur freedom to express their wildest food fantasies and serve the kind of people who these fantasies appeal to. The business model is pretty straightforward: Offer a specialty that won't break the bank, make it delicious (this is where your creativity comes into play), and whip it up in the shortest amount of time.

Nevertheless, many foodpreneurs have tried and tested this model without success. This shows that having an understanding of the model alone will not guarantee a profitable food truck business. Besides the cheap food, secret recipe, and outstanding customer service, you will need to have solid processes put in place that are applied and followed religiously!

This book introduces aspiring entrepreneurs, restaurateurs, and foodies who are looking to make a business out of their passion for food to the ins and outs of planning, establishing, and running a thriving food truck business. Think of this book as the ultimate beginner's guide that will set you up to succeed in your small food business. You may be thinking of starting a food truck as your next side hustle or perhaps a food truck business is your ticket out of the corporate world and into entrepreneurship. We all have dreams of bidding farewell to the traditional nine-to-five, but after reading this book, you may find that your dream can be a reality.

And if it means anything, the advice you receive in this book comes from two underdogs who started from the bottom and built successful businesses from the ground up. Even though there were times where we lacked capital, there was never a time where we lacked the sheer willpower to succeed.

From a young age, Walter Grant built "random things" out of scrap materials, just for the sake of it. His creativity never escaped him, and later on, he would go on to starting two businesses. His first business flunked, but this didn't derail him from his goal of becoming a successful businessman. A few years later—armed with a lot more experience and wisdom—he started his second business which he eventually sold for multiple eight figures!

And as for me? Well, I'm Andrew Hudson, and I'm what you call a typical foodie. Although, I would prefer the title of "inventor" since I have had many late nights creating extraordinary food art in the kitchen! I started my first food business when I was only 10 years old. It was a lemonade stand that my mother helped me set up. After graduating from college, and going through a few dead-end jobs, I decided to take the route less traveled and open my own food truck business.

Like many other young entrepreneurs, I didn't really know what I was going into, hence my first food truck business failed. But I had found my passion, and I wasn't going to quit anytime soon! I decided I would take another shot at it—this time doing my research and even seeking mentorship from successful foodpreneurs. Within a few months, business was booming; today, I have multiple food trucks stationed across America—all practically running on autopilot.

Now, it's your turn to build your food truck empire. But first, you will need to learn how to build a single food truck business from scratch. Do you think you're up for the challenge? Alright, that's the spirit! Turn over the page, and let's ride together on this journey!

CHAPTER 1
A DAY IN THE LIFE OF A FOOD TRUCK OWNER

I t's 5:00 a.m. and the alarm clock rings. That's my cue to wake up and prepare for what will be an eventful day. For the next hour, I tap into beast mode: I hit the gym for a 30-minute session; take a 20-minute shower and put on my chef's attire; and spend the last 10 minutes enjoying a power breakfast. Now, it's minutes past 7:00 a.m., and I'm about to head out to fetch my truck. But before I leave, I check what's on the menu for today. Since my business partners and I own several food trucks, we like to switch up the menus and give our customers something different every now and again.

From the looks of things, it looks like we're serving waffles, gourmet burgers, and hot dogs for lunch—the three signature meals that got us our first $100,000 in profits. Back then, we weren't used to making such large revenue, especially off of just three recipes! I head over to my kitchen; prepare the meats, spices, and greens; and neatly stock them in crates. My wife is already waiting for me in the car. She's my unassigned driver who drops me off at the truck depot early in the morning and fetches me in the evenings. Even though she isn't on our payroll, I reward her with mouthwatering dinners on most nights.

If I had a yard or a big enough garage, I would keep my truck at my place. But unfortunately, I live in the city, and finding space for trucks is near impossible. After I pick up the food truck, the first stop I make is to my local baker, Mr. Wang. Him and I go way back, and he's been a good support for my food truck business. The second stop is to the gas station to refill gas and my generator. (It's important to make sure the truck has enough fuel to get me around.) By the time the truck is loaded and ready to go, the time is around 10:00 a.m., and I have about two hours to prepare my meals before hungry customers arrive.

The location where my food truck is stationed is nearby and easily accessible to my customers. I park my truck near a local park, which is close to office blocks and schools. My typical customers are workers who come on their lunch breaks and moms who swing by either before or after they pick up their kids from school. Once all the preparations have been made, I signal that we're open for business by putting up my flap. Within several minutes, pedestrians come swooping in. Some of them are loyal customers coming to pick up their preorders, and others are new customers who are drawn by the aroma coming from the truck that travels down the entire street.

There are at least 15 to 20 people lining up outside the truck at any particular time. The lines remain full constantly throughout the day. At around 4:00 p.m., I put the flap down and close up my shop for the day. This is never easy for me to do because it means having to turn some customers away. However, I know that my customers are probably on their way home, and I need to clean up! Okay, I'll admit that this is the not-so-pretty part of the job. The cleanup involves scrubbing my grill and pots and cleaning my prep station and floor. If I have any leftover ingredients, I wrap them up and store them in the fridge or put them back in my crates.

The only thing left for me to do is head back to the depot. I usually arrive at the depot at 6:30 p.m. and find my wife waiting for me. I offload my crates and anything else that needs to remain refrigerated overnight. After locking up the truck, we head home, and the rest of my night is spent curled up on the couch with my wife and kids. Needless to say, I'm often physically exhausted when I get home. Depending on how much money I made that day, I may even feel a little frustrated. But since I'm passionate about this business, and I have the support of my family, I go to bed as a happy man and look forward to doing it all over again the next day!

IS THE FOOD TRUCK BUSINESS FOR ME?

When people go into business, their main objective is to make money. When researching the most popular food businesses in the U.S., you will mostly find food options, like pizza places or ice cream shops, ranking high. These are traditionally profitable businesses with profit margins between 20–35%; that's impressive considering that most traditional food shops make margins between 5–10% (Lee, 2019). However, since there is such a high demand for these kinds of shops in every city or town, it often means two things: First, you will need to buy large volumes of food and second, you will need to perform better than the other 50 pizza or ice cream shops in your district.

It still surprises me that food truck businesses haven't yet made it on the lists of most profitable food businesses. Granted, the food truck industry is relatively new, and before it was formalized, it was regarded as an informal food trade that a few free-spirited entrepreneurs were interested in. But if we look at the performance of food truck businesses, we can clearly see that the profits are either on par or better than what you'd make owning a physical food shop. Profit margins in this business are currently between 6–9%, but ultimately, the success of your food truck business depends on how much time and effort you invest into it.

While the margins are similar to that of a traditional restaurant, running a food truck business requires less capital and exposes you to fewer risks. Here are five reasons why a food truck is a better investment than starting your brick-and-mortar restaurant:

1. Food Trucks Require Lower Up-Front Costs

What makes a food truck business profitable is the fact there is lower initial capital required from you before you start making money. The average start-up cost for a restaurant is $275,000 or $3,046 per seat in a leased building. If you decide to purchase the building, the start-up costs increase (Sage, 2019). In contrast, you will only need between $28,000 and $114,000 to get your food truck running (CardConnect, n.d.). Leasing a truck may reduce your start-up costs, but nowadays, you can get a used truck for between $40,000 to $80,000. Later on in the book, I will give you strategies for reducing your food truck start-up costs even further!

2. Food Trucks Often Have Lower Operational Costs

There is a difference between start-up costs and operational costs. Start-up costs refer to the initial money you spend in order to get your business off the ground, but operational costs refer to the money you spend on a monthly basis to keep your business afloat. Both traditional restaurants and food trucks have operational costs, but the expenses of a food truck are significantly less than those of a restaurant. Of course, one food truck owner's expenses won't be the same as another. However, some of the expenses food truck owners don't have to pay include salaries for a full team of restaurant staff, property taxes, and other maintenance and security costs.

3. Food Trucks Attract More Business

There's a reason consumers are obsessed with food trucks. Who wouldn't want exotic food that you could only dream up, served within a matter of minutes, and at half the price of restaurant food? In traditional restaurants, gourmet meals tend to have a hefty price point, but this isn't the case with meals from food trucks. They are budget-friendly and prepared with the same quality as meals cooked in restaurants. Food from food trucks is also considered safer and more hygienic than food prepared by informal street vendors. This appeals to the new kind of foodie who enjoys exploring new flavors but remains health conscious.

4. Food Trucks Aren't Restricted by Location

Once you have signed a lease for a building, you are tied to your lease agreement until the period is over. This can pose a serious risk, especially when the restaurant owner hasn't done a comprehensive market analysis, and as a result, they chose an unpopular location for their target consumers. Food trucks give owners the freedom of testing out different locations before settling at the best one. There are some locations where a license or parking fee is required, but for the most part, food trucks have access to a wide range of public spaces. If your business model isn't a match with your desired location, you can explore the city and find another suitable location.

5. Food Trucks Give You Room to Grow Your Brand

If you have dreams of one day owning a chain of restaurants, you can build your brand by first opening a food truck and establishing your customer base. Alternatively, you might decide to expand your brand by owning a chain of food trucks and setting up in strategic places in your state or in multiple states. You have a lot more room to express your creative ideas with a food truck, from customizing your truck in your brand colors and logo to creating signature dishes and one-of-a-kind experiences. Plus, since your business is quite literally a "billboard on wheels," you spend less money on advertising than a restaurant in a fixed location.

CHALLENGES OF OWNING A FOOD TRUCK

Every business owner experiences their own fair share of headaches when it comes to operating a successful business. The food truck business is no different. Although, unlike restaurant owners, food truck owners find themselves with a unique set of challenges:

1. Food Trucks Need to Comply with Local Laws and Regulations

As simple as the business model is for operating a food truck, owners still need to get the green light from local officials before they can start serving customers. In the U.S., this process can be complicated because each state, city, and county has its own set of policies regulating food trucks. Owners must consult a local official and complete the necessary paperwork before operating their business. Some of the common permits and certification required include:

- Certificate from the health department
- Food safety training
- A seller's permit
- Permits for the truck (including driver's license, registration, and inspection documents)
- Mobile vending laws
- Liability insurance

2. Food Trucks Deal with Parking Issues

In many locations, food truck owners aren't allowed to park wherever they want. You're in a good position when you rent a spot at a food truck park because then all you will need to pay is a parking fee. If you station your food truck at a farmer's market or festival, you may need to pay a fee for your spot or give them a percentage of your sales. It's also wise not to target places with heavy traffic or where the roads are narrow, and your truck is likely to create obstructions for other drivers.

3. Food Trucks Can't Store Bulk Amounts of Food

The key to serving customers quality food in the shortest amount of time is food preparation. This means that you should plan ahead of time how many meals you will serve, and the ingredients needed to prepare the meals each day. Food truck owners don't have the luxury of storing large amounts of food in large refrigerators like restaurants do. To produce fresh meals every day, the owner will need to have a long grocery list of ingredients on hand, carefully calculated to prepare X number of meals.

4. Food Truck Owners Have to Consider the Weather

Regardless of how much preparation you can do or how attractive your truck looks from the outside, your revenue for the day can be affected by the weather. Customers are less likely to come out in the rain and stand in a line to buy a meal. They would rather order in and get food delivered to their home or office block. Food trucks parked at festivals or farmers' markets may also receive less business when the weather isn't good.

5. Food Truck Owners Must Be Good Drivers

Have you seen the size of an average food truck? Food trucks are usually between 14 to 35 feet long and 7 feet wide (Karpatia Trucks, 2020). Of course, the size of your food truck will be determined by many factors, such as how many employees you will have, how many people you will serve, and what you plan on cooking. Nonetheless, you will need to have a truck driving license and understand the mechanics of your large vehicle, so you can get from one location to the next with ease, park your truck properly, and respond promptly when your vehicle needs repairs.

WHAT ARE MY OTHER OPTIONS?

You might love the idea of a mobile food business but aren't sold on the food truck idea, or perhaps you cannot afford to buy a truck right now. Fortunately, food trucks aren't the only option when it comes to selling food on wheels. Here are a few alternatives to food trucks:

1. Concession Trailers

Concession trailers have been around for many years and are used as an alternative to food trucks at outdoor functions, festivals, or fairs. The difference between a food truck and a concession trailer is that the latter doesn't have a built-in engine. This means that you need to have another vehicle with enough power to carry the trailer on the road. The advantage with using a trailer is that it isn't likely to break down or need repairs as much as a food truck. Moreover, since it doesn't have an engine, trailers are typically more affordable compared to food trucks.

2. Food Vans

Food vans are standard vehicles that are converted into mobile kitchens. These vans range in size, price, and models; common examples include the Mercedes-Benz Sprinter, the Ford Transit, or the Ram ProMaster cargo van (M&R, 2018). The only drawback when using these vehicles is that you have a limited amount of space to work in. If you are thinking of hiring help in the kitchen, a maximum of two people can fit comfortably inside the van. Nevertheless, the size of these vehicles make them ideal if you live in a busy city, and models like the Mercedes-Benz Sprinter can handle a fair amount of the daily wear and tear that comes with running a food operation.

3. Food Carts

Food carts were made famous by the hot dog, ice cream, and pretzel stands that appeared across major cities in the U.S. Even though these count as food carts, the latest inventions in food carts allow you to serve more customers and prepare more complex meals. For instance, if you love barbecue, you might want to consider getting a barbecue grill and smoker that can be easily transported from a farmer's market or concert venue to another. Modern-day food carts come with a variety of features that give you the option of starting your own catering or food business.

4. Shipping Containers

Another relatively new trend is converting shipping containers into mobile kitchens. A shipping container can easily fit at the back of a truck and be carried from one location to another, although containers are perfect when your store operates in a permanent location (such as being based in farmers' markets). What makes this option attractive is that shipping containers are low cost, durable, and come in different sizes. Similar to food trucks, containers give you a lot of flexibility when designing it to resemble your brand.

5. Catering Business

Lastly, if you are still unsure about a food truck business, you can start off with a catering business. The model for catering businesses is slightly different, but it is still considered a mobile food business. For instance, you aren't required to have a food vehicle. All you will need is access to a commercial kitchen, the right serving equipment, and a catering license.

CHAPTER 2
LAYING THE
FOUNDATION

You probably have a lot of questions regarding the process of running a successful food truck. All of your questions (and those of your funders, if you are planning on going the financing route) can be answered in one comprehensive document, known as a business plan. There are many entrepreneurs who don't see the necessity of a business plan. They believe that it's a useless document that will only take up their time. From my own experiences starting businesses, I can tell you that skipping the business plan will cost you more money and time in the future.

There is a famous saying: Failing to plan is planning to fail. In my own life, I have found this saying to be true. A business plan allows you to cover all of your bases and predict possible risks or challenges in the future that may negatively impact your business. A business plan also gives you a sober outlook on your business and details exactly what you need to do on a weekly, monthly, or yearly basis to succeed. There are no shortcuts in growing a six-figure business, and if you are in a hurry, you may build an unstable foundation. Give yourself enough time to conduct thorough research on your food truck business and compile a business plan, which must be treated as a working document (being able to make edits and updates whenever circumstances call for it).

NINE COMPONENTS OF A BUSINESS PLAN

All business plans, despite the type of business or industry, will include nine components: executive summary, company overview, industry analysis, customer analysis, competitive analysis, marketing plan, operations plan, management team, and the financial plan. How each component is explained will differ for each business, depending on its unique brand, value proposition, and model. Below is an explanation of each component and an example of how it would like for a food truck business:

1. Executive Summary

An executive summary appears within the first few pages of your business plan—after your cover page and table of contents. It summarizes the information contained in the business plan in about three to five paragraphs (about a page in length). Funders are likely to look at your executive summary first before reading any further. Thus, it's important that you include the key points that sell your business and give prospective investors or lenders enough information about your start-up. Your food truck executive summary should include the following points:

- The name of the business and what type of business it is
- The food items you plan to sell and specialize in
- The key people or partners that will manage the business
- The basic marketing plan that the business will implement (You don't have to give too many details away.)
- Projected start-up capital needed to get the business up and running (as well as the people who will fund the business during the start-up stage)
- The long-term vision for your food truck business— where you see it in the next 5–10 years.

Here is an example of an executive summary:

The Mobile Juice Laboratory, located in West Hollywood, is a health-conscious food truck focused on providing organic and freshly prepared juices and smoothies. Our product fits well with the health trends nationwide but particularly in Los Angeles, where individuals are

constantly looking for low-fat, vegan-friendly natural foods on the go.

The Mobile Juice Laboratory is founded by Jenna Michells who has run a mail order juice company for over 10 years. While she has never run a food truck before, she hopes that it will be a great way to expand her business and reach more customers around the area.

Some of the opportunities for the company are that there are no other upscale mobile juicing companies in West Los Angeles at the moment, and the business already has a recognizable brand that is loved by its loyal customers. The company will make use of its social media channels, monthly product specials, and new smoothie recipes to attract new customers.

The Mobile Juice Laboratory is seeking $250,000 as start-up funding to launch its new food truck. These funds will be used to purchase a used truck, design the mobile kitchen, and invest in a 12-month social media campaign. In five years' time, The Mobile Juice Laboratory will become the preferred store for healthy juices and smooth-ies, as well as other healthy meals that will be launched in year two.

2. Company Overview

The next component is the company overview. Here, you will need to answer three questions:

1. What is your company?

2. How many years have you been in the industry (or what experience do you have in the industry)?

3. What products do you offer?

If you have been in the food industry for a while, it would be great to start off with your company history. If your business is new, you can begin by explaining your business concept. While your executive summary needs to be formal, your company overview should be written in the same style and language as your brand.

You can also include your mission statement. This can be a few sentences or a short paragraph defining what you plan to serve, who you plan to serve, as well as the ultimate vision of your business. Your mission statement isn't just something nice to have; it should be what you live by. A powerful mission statement can be a source of encouragement and influence how you operate your business. Here is an example of a mission statement:

To provide residents of Los Angeles, both young and old, with organic juices and healthy smoothies that support a healthy lifestyle. We use 100% fresh and local ingredients and provide vegan-friendly, gluten-free, and low-fat products for the ideal health-conscious customer.

3. **Industry Analysis**

An industry analysis (or market analysis) describes the size and performance of the market the business is operating in as well as some key market players. For smaller markets, like the food truck industry, there won't be a lot of market research available or many major rivals that you will be competing with. Your industry analysis will also depend on where your business is located. In larger cities, the market for food trucks may be large, and there may be several food truck businesses that have built reputable brands.

In this section, you will also want to identify the type of food trucks that already exist and the type of customers that support these food trucks. This will allow you to identify gaps in product offerings (you can serve customers foods that aren't already being offered) and appeal to new kinds of customers that may have not been considered (like stay-at-home moms, construction workers, college students, etc.). Use recent market data to identify local trends that you can capitalize on.

4. Customer Analysis

Once you have completed your industry analysis, you will have sufficient knowledge about your ideal customer. In this section, you will need to conduct a demographic profile of your target market. Some of the factors you will need to consider include:

- Population size
- Predicted population growth

- Age group
- Gender ratio (how many genders in comparison)
- Income bracket
- Interests, preferences, and lifestyle choices

After you have compiled a demographic profile of your target market, you can create customer segments. These are subgroups that your target market falls under, based on unique characteristics, life stages, and lifestyle choices. The broader your target market is, the more customer segments you will have. For example, if your target market includes people living in Los Angeles, you could have the following customer segments:

The soccer mom: Stay-at-home mothers who are active in the community and in their children's educational careers. These women tend to have busy schedules and juggle home and school life. During the day, they often go to gym, run errands, or meet with other soccer moms for lunch.

Local office workers: Professionals working in nearby offices and buildings. Their work weeks are intense, and lunch is always eaten on the go. They tend to be highly stressed individuals who are looking for convenient meals that are healthy and can provide them with the necessary energy to continue working throughout the day.

Families and couples: There are many community areas in Los Angeles where families and couples live. They prefer to be seen out and about at the best restaurants and streets in L.A. During the day, while running errands or shopping, they appreciate a healthy, light meal that is prepared with restaurant quality.

5. Competitive Analysis

You might think that just because there isn't another food truck in your neighborhood that you don't have any competitors. Well, this is not exactly true. We can divide competitors into two groups: direct and indirect competitors. Direct competitors are businesses that offer identical or similar products as you. They may be other food trucks, food carts, or catering businesses—essentially, any mobile food business. Indirect competitors are businesses that offer products that are close but in a different category. These may be traditional restaurants or fast food companies.

When creating your competitive analysis, you will need to drive around town, go on social media, speak to a few people, and find out which other direct or indirect competitors are operating in your city. Do some research on your competitors and find out what products they offer, the type of customers they serve, and their general business model. Once you have compiled research on your competitors, write down their strengths and weaknesses. The strengths are usually the things your competitors excel at (and are really tough to compete with), and the weaknesses are the things your competitors have either overlooked or aren't good at. Here is an example of how you would analyze a competitor:

Organic Haven is a healthy food store that serves ready-made healthy meals. They specialize in healthy breakfast meals and breakfast snacks, but have very limited options when it comes to lunch and dinner options. Organic Haven does not make smoothies or healthy juices which gives us a competitive advantage. Moreover, the store opened six months ago, and they are still building their customer base, whereas we have established long-term relationships with many of our customers.

Your competitive analysis can even include your competitor's pricing for various food products. Your best bet is to try and price your goods at the same point or a little lower than your competitors, but there will be more on pricing strategies later in the book!

6. Marketing Plan

Your marketing plan has one main objective: to build a loyal customer base. The content of your plan will include various strategies on how you will appeal to the needs and desires of your customers and position your brand in a favorable light. An important thing to remember is that customers are bombarded with hundreds of brands trying to sell them products and services on a daily basis. To stand out from the crowd, you will need to offer them something different, whether it means having a unique brand identity or selling exotic meals. Here are a few questions that you can ask yourself when creating your marketing plan:

How are you going to compete with other food trucks in your area? Are you planning on setting prices lower than your competitors? Do you plan on offering new products that haven't been seen before?

How are you going to grow your business? Will you hire employees to help you in the kitchen? Will you invest in more food trucks? Do you plan on attending several fairs and festivals throughout the year?

How will you distribute your product? Is your food truck the only way customers can get a hold of your products? Will you attend food festivals and events?

How will you get across to your customers? Do you plan on advertising on radio, the local newspaper, or TV? Will you create social media accounts for your business and pay for social media advertising? Will you offer daily, weekly, or monthly discounts on selected food products? Will you entice prospective customers by offering free samples? Will you have a grand opening/launch?

How many meals must you sell each day or every week for your food truck business to be profitable? What would be a fair menu price for your products? How many hours per day and days per week will you operate? How many rest days will you give yourself (or your staff) a month? Will you work during public holidays? Will your food truck sell throughout winter or only in summer months?

7. Operations Plan

An operations plan explains the detailed processes and systems the business will need to follow on a daily basis in order to succeed. Once an operations plan has been put in motion, it creates predictable outcomes for the business. This is good because it means that you can manage costs and stay on track to meeting your weekly and monthly targets! Your operational plan will need to consider a variety of factors that make your food truck run smoothly. Some of these factors include:

Functional roles of staff: Who is going to perform various functions in your business, like driving, administrative work, handling the finances, marketing, cooking, and so on?

Assets: What assets will you need to run your food truck? How will you protect and maintain these assets?

Product: How many recipes will your menu include? Who is in charge of preparing these recipes? Where will you source the ingredients? How many ingredients will you need for a day's worth of meals?

Finances: Who will handle your business finances? Will you collect money in cash or offer other payment options to customers?

Milestones: What are your company milestones? What are the plans you have put in place to achieve these milestones? How many times will you review your milestones?

Routes: Where will your food truck be based? What permits and certification do you need to park your truck in that particular location? What are the best days of the week or times of day to open your food truck at that location? What is the best route of getting to your location during the week and on weekends? How much fuel will you need in your truck every day or week? Will you need a backup generator?

8. Management Team

This section is straightforward. You would list all of the people who work for your company, starting from the founders to the interns. Introduce each person and give a brief outline of their qualifications and experience in their respective role. If your food truck is a one-man show, you can describe yourself as the founder, driver, cook, and any other capacity you will be operating in. Make sure that you also outline each person's set of responsibilities on the document so that later down the line, you can revert back to the plan when there is conflict over tasks and expectations. If you haven't recruited employees yet, you can create a hiring plan that includes the number of staff needed, whether they will work full time or part time, and the level of experience required.

9. Financial Plan

Even though the financial plan tends to come at the end of the document, it is one of the most crucial components of your business plan. If you are a new food truck business, your financial plan will consist of projected income and expenses you believe your business will generate over a specific period. Since these are projections, ensure that you don't make the figures up in your head but that you do thorough calculations based on realistic assumptions. The purpose of your financial plan is to prove that your business will be profitable. From a practical perspective, you will want to assess the break-even point (the point where you are neither making a loss or a profit) of your business. In other words: How many meals will I need to sell every month to pay off all of my expenses?

Here's a quick formula for working out your break-even point:

Fixed Costs/(Sales Price per Unit - Variable Costs per Unit) = Break-Even Point

Add up your projected monthly expenses from your food truck to get your fixed costs. Make sure that you only include items that you pay on a recurring basis, such as your loan payments, insurance, salaries, gas, cell phone, etc.

The "Sales Price Per Unit" refers to how much you plan on charging your customers for a product the calculation is being done for.

Variable costs are different from operational costs in the sense that they are the costs specifically associated with the production of a product, from buying the ingredients to preparing and packaging it. Variable costs tend to fluctuate, so give a rough estimate. To calculate variable costs per unit, you would take your total variable costs and divide the figure by the total units produced.

The calculation will show you how many sales of a particular product you will need to make to reach your break-even point. Look at the final number. Is it something attainable for your start-up business? If not, you may need to find a more affordable product to sell, reduce the variable costs associated with producing your product (you don't need expensive food wrapping paper), or find a way to reduce your monthly expenses (perhaps you can lease a truck rather than purchasing a brand new one).

When making financial projections, focus on the first 12 months. Your calculations over a 12-month period will most likely be more accurate than your calculations over a five-year period. Plus, you will refer to your financial plan a lot during the first year, so make sure your numbers are a true representation of what the first year will look like financially. Working out projected income may take some guesswork, but you can speak to local food truck owners and ask them how much money they make a month and work on those figures. Determining your projected expenses will be a lot simpler since you will likely have the same expenses every month. While there may be unexpected expenses that pop up randomly, these don't occur often. Having a savings tool like an emergency fund can help you settle those unexpected (and cruel) expenses that eat away at your profits!

CHAPTER 3
PLAYING BY THE RULES

W hat is one of the biggest hurdles you will need to jump as a food truck owner? Getting your permits, so you can begin operating your business! As tedious as this process is, careful planning and doing your research beforehand will speed up the process. Depending on the state you live in, you will need to obtain certain licenses and permits. Check in with your local authorities and business councils about the various licenses and permits you will need to legalize your business.

COMMON LICENSES AND PERMITS REQUIRED FOR FOOD TRUCK BUSINESSES

While licenses and permits vary from one state, city, or county to another, here are some of the common licenses and permits required for food truck businesses:

1. Business License

A business license, or business operation license, is a permit you will need to run a food truck business in your local district. This permit helps the government identify what type of business you have and enables it to track the operations of your business for tax purposes. A business license also legitimizes your operations and proves your credibility to the general public. Check in with your local business registrar to ding out the additional documentation and fees you need to pay to secure a business license.

2. Employer Identification Number (EIN)

If you plan on hiring staff, even if it's part time, you will need to complete an EIN application. This will grant you a federal tax ID, issued by the IRS, which allows you to open a business account with a bank and build your business credit profile. If you decide to be the sole person running your business, it is still advised to apply for an EIN because after incorporating the business, the owner is typically seen as an employee of the business.

3. Parking Permit

Many neighborhoods won't allow food trucks to park on the side of the road for extended periods of time. Moreover, many cities have certain zoning laws that place restrictions on where food trucks can park which you will need to adhere to. It's safer to obtain a parking permit for your food truck and get a printed sheet of the various locations your truck is not allowed to park at. It's also wise to ask about other parking rules, such as how close you are allowed to park to brick-and-mortar restaurants offering similar foods, where you are allowed to store your truck overnight, or whether you are expected to pay parking meters.

4. Health Permit

If you are planning on operating in the food industry, you will need to pass the health and safety standards before selling food. The health department in your state may want to inspect your food truck and require documents about your health and safety procedures before giving you clearance; you can add your health and safety procedures in the "Operations plan" section of your business plan. Operating without a health permit can reflect poorly on your business and make customers doubt the quality of your food and cleanliness of your food truck. It's also worth noting that a health permit is just the bare minimum when it comes to ensuring the health and safety of your operation. After you get your health permit, you can apply for a food handlers permit (for the chef who will be handling the food) and a mobile food facility permit. Ensure that you renew your health permit on a regular basis.

5. Vehicle License for Food Truck

Your food truck will also need to have its own vehicle license up to date. If you are buying a used truck, make sure that the vehicle has passed its roadworthy tests and that all of its fines have been paid and cleared. Your driver's license will also need to be up to date and appropriate for the kind of vehicle you are driving. Depending on the weight of your truck, you may need to have a commercial driver's license to legally drive the vehicle. Check in with the Department of Motor Vehicles (DMV) for licensing requirements.

EXAMPLE OF LICENSES REQUIRED IN MAJOR U.S. CITIES

It's common to find food trucks operating in major cities across the U.S. Here are a few licenses that you will be required to obtain in various cities (Krook, 2019):

License Checklist for New York City

- Mobile food vendor personal license ($74–$200)
- Mobile food vending unit permit (each truck will need to have its own permit) ($15–$200)
- NYC Department of Health and Mental Hygiene permit ($280 plus $25 if you make frozen desserts)

- New York state tax permit and certificate (no fee, although it must be filed on a quarterly basis)
- Food handling certificate ($25)
- Employer Identification Number (free if you file it yourself)
- Driver's license and registration ($140–$180)

Note: In New York City, there is usually a long waiting list for the food vendor permit. To save time, food truck owners can apply for a restricted area permit in the meantime. This permit allows you to operate in and around parks but not on the roads.

License Checklist for Los Angeles

- Business tax certificate (must be obtained from the Office of Finance; no fee is charged)
- Public health operating license (must be obtained from the L.A. County Department of Public Health; costs between $150–$$600+)
- Licensed commissary rental or ownership (commissaries are commercial kitchen spaces where you can prepare or store food; rental ranges between $500–$1,500 per truck per month)
- Manager's food safety certification (required for the food truck owner and kitchen staff; costs $99 per person and includes a course that comes with an exam)
- Food handlers permit ($7 per person)

- Employer Identification Number (free if you file it yourself)
- Driver's license and registration ($110–$260)

Note: It's required, according to California law, that all food trucks have access to a commissary (either rented or owned). The commissary must be approved by the specific county's department of public health. Food trucks not only prepare food at commissaries, but they can also store food and keep their food trucks parked overnight.

License Checklist for Chicago

- Mobile food license (registered as either a mobile food dispenser or mobile food preparer; costs between $700–$1,000 for a two-year term)
- Retail food establishment or shared kitchen user business license ($330–$660 per shared kitchen or user)
- City of Chicago food sanitation manager certificate ($40)
- Fire safety permit (only required if your truck has a gas or electric generator, propane, a fire suppression hood, or compressed natural gas)
- Employer Identification Number (free if you file it yourself)
- Driver's license and registration ($200–$250)

Note: The mobile food license fee will depend on the kinds of foods you plan on serving on your food truck and whether you plan on cooking them in your truck or at a commissary. Moreover, according to Illinois State Law, food truck owners aren't allowed to prepare or store food intended for commercial use in a home kitchen (Krook, 2019). Therefore, if your food truck is based in Illinois, you will need to rent or own a licensed commissary in Chicago.

License Checklist for Austin

- Mobile food vendor permit (restricted or unrestricted; costs between $420–$500)
- City of Austin food manager certificate (at least one person in your business should have one; costs between $32–$85)
- State-approved food handlers training course certificate/s (required for every employee that will be handling food; costs between $7–$10 per person)
- Registered Central Preparation Facility (CPF) certificate (this is an agreement you enter with your commissary; costs $150)
- Employer Identification Number (free if you file it yourself)
- Driver's license and registration ($60–$75)

Note: A restricted mobile food vendor permit only allows you to sell prepackaged products which means you can't prepare food in your truck. The unrestricted mobile food vendor permit allows you to sell prepackaged foods plus prepare meals in your truck.

HOW TO OBTAIN A FOOD ESTABLISHMENT PERMIT FOR YOUR FOOD TRUCK

There are four general steps that every food truck owner must follow to get their food establishment permit for their food truck (or other mobile food unit) approved. Note that the steps below outline the process required for food truck owners operating in Fairfax County, Virginia, but they can give you a general understanding of how the process of obtaining a permit goes (Fairfax County, n.d.):

Step 1: Submit Your Food Truck Plans for Review

Your food truck plans are the architectural drawings of the layout of your mobile food unit. These plans are submitted to the health department by any owner or builder who intends on remodeling or converting a vehicle to a mobile kitchen unit. The plans must comply with the specific requirements stipulated in the health department's guidelines for operating mobile food units. Moreover, the plans must be drawn to scale and include the schematic view of the equipment layout as well as the proposed plumbing and electrical installations and construction materials that will be used.

Step 2: Apply for a Food Permit

To apply for a food permit, you will need to complete a Mobile Food Unit Application, a Commissary Agreement for a Mobile Food Unit, and a Mobile Food Vending Zone Agreement. Get in touch with the health department on the requirements for completing these forms.

Step 3: Schedule a Preoccupancy Inspection

A preoccupancy inspection is done by appointment only. A member of the U.S. Department of Health does an inspection of your mobile food unit, assessing whether the unit complies with the local regulations regarding food trucks or similar units. A certified food manager representing your company must be present during the inspection (this can be the food truck owner or one of the employees). During the inspection, the official will ask you to provide the following:

- The food permit application (if it hasn't been submitted already)
- Copies of the certified food manager's licenses for every individual who works with food in the truck
- The business name written in three inch lettering on both sides of the vehicle
- Approved sanitizer and test kit
- A three compartment sink (if required) with a faucet reaching over all compartments of the sink (the faucet must pour out hot and cold water)

- A hand sink with a soap dispenser and disposable hand towels
- Approved probe thermometer
- NSF-approved equipment
- If the mobile food unit is stationed in a permanent location, like a building, a lease agreement with the building owner is required.

Step 4: Prepare to Open for Business!

After you pass your preoccupancy inspection and all of the construction, safety, and equipment requirements have been approved, a permit and decal will be issued by the U.S. Department of Health. You can finally prepare to open your business!

FIVE ORGANIZATIONAL TIPS FOR PREPARING YOUR PAPERWORK

You don't have to be discouraged by all the paperwork involved in getting your food truck business started. Here are a few organizational tips that can help you get through the process efficiently:

1. Use Checklists

Keeping mental notes won't help you remember all of the small and major permits you need to apply for. Get yourself a notebook and write down a list of all the permits and licenses you need to submit and get approval for. Order the items on your checklist from the most important to the least important. Tackle items that have longer waiting periods first so that you can work on other paperwork while waiting for approval. Lastly, reward yourself every time you cross off an item on your list!

2. Dedicate Time for Research

While I have tried to give you as much information on the permits and licenses required to register your food truck, there may be special permits that I forgot to mention. Make time to do your own comprehensive research and call your local health department to verify your information. Scheduling time for research ensures that there are no other commitments that take up your time. You can decide to spend 20 minutes every evening gathering information or dedicate an entire weekend to getting it done.

3. Keep Records of Your Meetings and Emails

It's important to keep record of the engagements you have had with local officials and the various status emails that tell you how far along your applications are or why your submission was rejected. Keeping record helps you track your progress and allows you to see how much information you still need to gather. Your records can also protect you when there seems to be a misunderstanding between you and officials. For example, if you fail to file for a permit because an official told you that you don't need to have it, you can show proof of that email exchange so that you can prove it was a misunderstanding.

4. Keep All Your Documents in One Place

This simple tip can make your application process run a lot smoother. It's easy for notes and printouts to get lost among other forms and papers. Thus, you must designate an area in your office cupboard or desk where you store all of your business-related paperwork. Knowing where to look for certain documents will save you time and help you determine outstanding documents quickly. If the applications ask for you to submit physical copies, scan your hard copies so that you don't mistakenly submit the original documents.

5. Use the Same Personal Information Every Time

When completing forms, remember to use the same personal information on every document. This ensures that there are no discrepancies in your applications. For instance, decide whether you will add your second name or not, which email address you would like them to contact you on, and the correct home address format. When writing down your business name, use the official business registration name—not the shortened version. Using the same personal information also allows you to fill in forms a lot quicker.

CHAPTER 4
ASSOCIATED COSTS AND WHERE TO GET FUNDING

O ne of the main reasons start-up entrepreneurs are drawn to food trucks is because it has low start-up costs. Don't take this to mean that you won't be required to invest any substantial money in the beginning, but what you end up investing won't be as much as other types of food businesses. Calculating your start-up costs will require you to do your own research and speak to a number of vendors. Fortunately, this chapter will give you an overview of all the costs involved, so you can start looking at possible funding options!

THE COST BREAKDOWN FOR RUNNING A FOOD TRUCK

Starting a food truck business is affordable but not cheap. Here are some of the start-up costs you can expect to pay:

1. The Food Truck = $15,000 - $150,000

There wouldn't be a food truck business without a food truck. Purchasing a truck (whether it's new or used) will be one of your largest expenses. The good news is that you have a wide range of vehicle models and dealers to choose from, so you can end up paying at the low end of your budget. Used food trucks will be at the low end of your budget, costing around $50,000. However, like any used vehicle, a used food truck may come with unique faults. Put some money away for possible repair costs so that you aren't caught by surprise when the vehicle needs servicing. It's also worth noting that banks will charge you a higher loan interest rate when you purchase a used vehicle rather than a brand new one.

New food trucks will be at the higher end of your budget and will cost you between $75,000 and $150,000. While you will pay a lot more money up front, you are almost guaranteed to not find any faults with your vehicle, plus, you will have a valid warranty). The final price you end up paying for your new food truck will depend on the size of the unit, the features inside the unit, and any customization or branding that you pay for. If you can't afford to purchase a used or new truck, there is also the option of leasing a truck. Leasing a food truck can cost you between $2,000 to $3,000 per month. The upside with leasing a truck is that you don't have to apply for a car loan or pay maintenance costs on your vehicle. Many leased food trucks come with a commissary kitchen included in the fee, saving you about $1,000 in fees.

2. The Kitchen Inventory = $3,488 - $6,303

Your food truck will come with a built-in kitchen, but you are expected to purchase kitchen tools and equipment. The type of kitchen equipment you will need depends on the kinds of foods you will be preparing. For example, if you are going to be making burgers and fries, you will need to have a grill, fryer, refrigerator, meat pounder, a set of knives, and so on. Other equipment may include pots, pans, utensils, and appliances like a microwave or food processor. When you are launching your business and still testing out your menu, it would be better to lease your kitchen equipment. You may find that certain products don't sell well and that you won't need a certain machine. Leasing equipment also gives you time to build capital, so you can reinvest in your business.

3. The Actual Food

So far, you have purchased a food truck, kitchen equipment, and now, you need to buy the food. Food costs will vary depending on the products you sell. Moreover, if you can find reasonable food suppliers who can cut you a deal, you can reduce your food costs even more. But assuming that you are going to buy your ingredients at a local grocery store, try to base your menu on seasonal ingredients or items that are always on special or priced low, like bread, fruits, and vegetables. Even though I cannot give you an estimate of how much your food will cost, I can show you how to do your own calculation.

First, you will need to decide on what you plan on serving customers and how many meals you will prepare a day. Let's say you decide on serving 100 meals a day for a full month (30 days). That would give you 3,000 total orders per month. Additionally, since you are starting up, let's say you decide to offer a limited menu of juicy burgers, fries, and soda. Next, you would need to go online and research how much preparing each ingredient will cost you. The following are estimates I found online:

• Burger (including bun, meat, vegetables, sauce, etc.) = $3.08 per serving (Priceonomics, 2017)

• Fries = 0.75¢ to $1 per 1-lb serving (based on $25 for a 30-lb box) (Howmuchisit Staff, 2018)

• Soda = $1.19 per 16 oz. Coca-Cola can (Hangover Staff, 2019)

For customers who order a combo, which includes all three items, you are looking at a cost of $5.02 per meal. For an entire month, this brings your total food cost to $15,060 (after fulfilling 3,000 orders). Of course, not every customer will purchase a combo meal, which means that your food costs may be less. However, if you stick to your target of 3,000 orders, you won't pay more than $15,060. Note that this figure does not include all of the other variable costs you will pay to produce your meals, such as the food wrapping, straws, and napkins.

4. Labor Costs

Besides the food truck, your other major expense will be labor costs. In general, labor costs make up between 25–35% of your total operating costs. Even if you plan on doing most of the cooking, you will need someone on the truck who can attend to customers at the front while you cook at the back. Or if you plan on running a large-scale operation at farmers' markets and festivals where there are hungry crowds of people to serve, you will need to have a few employees who can help you run your food truck. Labor costs vary depending on location; therefore, it's difficult to give an estimate here, too. You can reduce your labor costs by hiring family members to assist you on weekends, hiring newly graduated chefs from culinary school, or hiring employees who are qualified to handle multiple tasks.

5. Permits, Licenses, Parking, Insurance = $3,100–$6,900

As highlighted in the previous chapter, each permit or license comes with its own fee. Some permits are renewed each year, and others only charge a once-off fee. Set reminders for permits and licenses that are renewed yearly so that you don't incur any late penalties. Besides permits and licenses, you will need to insure your business and vehicle. Business insurance is necessary, especially because you will be handling food, and you wouldn't want any of your customers to sue you after falling sick from your food. You'll also want to insure your business against employee injuries while on the job, vehicle damage, property damage, and fire damage. Other miscellaneous costs include parking fees, commissary kitchen rental, gas, and event entrance fees.

6. Enough Working Capital to Last You the First Few Months

One of the most underrated costs of starting a business is working capital. Business owners invest so much money in buying assets that they forget about the daily and monthly costs of staying afloat. Since your business will be new, you can expect to spend more money than you earn in the first few months or until you reach your break-even point. This means that you will need to have a surplus of cash that can cover your monthly expenses while you slowly build your revenue stream. While it's good to expect a high turnover of customers, plan for the worst by having enough cash to support you when your turnover isn't that great.

SEEKING BUSINESS FUNDING

Now that you have an estimate of the amount of start-up capital you will need, you can now start thinking about potential sources of finance. The best-case scenario is if you have a lump sum of money in your savings account that you can use to get your food truck off the ground. Nevertheless, this option isn't viable for most people, so we need to consider other options. If you know of family members who would be willing to invest in your business, you could reach out to them and present your business plan. Otherwise, you may need to approach lenders and apply for a business loan. Below is a summary of all the options you can consider when seeking business funding:

1. Personal Savings

If you have money in your savings account, consider using some of it toward your start-up capital. The benefit of using your own cash is that you don't need to borrow money from lenders (or pay exorbitant interest rates). One of the main risks, however, is that if your business doesn't succeed, you lose all of the money you had invested into it.

2. Family and Friends

Another great source of funding is your network of friends and family. If you find someone who is interested, you can pitch them your idea and negotiate the financing deal. Someone might be willing to take out a business loan on your behalf and expect you to make repayments directly to them every month. Another person may be willing to give you capital in exchange for equity in your business. After you have reached an agreement, put it in writing and ensure that all of the parties' signatures are on the document. Even though you are familiar with your friend or relative, treat the agreement as a legally binding contract and honor the funding terms.

3. Rollover for Business Start-ups (ROBS)

Creating a ROBS gives you a legal way to access your retirement funds early without incurring penalties (Seppala, 2020). Before you can set up your ROBS, you must form a new C-corporation. Once your C-corporation has been established, you can set up a retirement plan for your C-corporation. Thereafter, you can transfer the funds from your existing retirement plan to your new retirement plan! You can use these funds toward working capital, purchasing food items, or paying for permits and license fees.

Before you can implement this strategy, there are a few things to note. First, you must be an employee of your newly formed corporation and comply with all the necessary business laws and regulations. You will also need to pay a setup fee directly to your ROBS provider as well as a monthly maintenance fee. The only other drawback to this strategy is that similar to using your personal savings, you risk losing your retirement savings if your business doesn't succeed.

4. Line of Credit

A line of credit is a type of loan that functions more like a credit card. Your lender will approve you for a certain amount of credit. This means that you can spend as much or as little money as you want—as long as it doesn't exceed your threshold. However, instead of withdrawing money using a credit card, you transfer money from your line of credit account into your business account. You are expected to repay the money you borrow through scheduled payments over a period of time.

5. Purchase Financing

If you need a loan to cover the costs of large assets and inventory, you can inquire about purchase financing. The lender purchases the assets, inventory, or equipment from your selected vendors, and then, you will spend the next few years repaying the lender for the total purchase of goods plus fees and interest charged.

6. Personal Loans for Business

Most lenders are skeptical of borrowing funds to small business entrepreneurs. They may ask you for tons of paperwork to prove the viability of your business or that you can afford to repay the loan should your business fail. However, you can bypass this hurdle by seeking a personal loan instead. Getting approved for a personal loan will depend significantly on your credit profile, credit history, and how much money you earn on a monthly basis. If you have debt, focus on paying some of it off on a consistent basis, so you can improve your credit score before applying for a personal loan. If you don't have debt, you may need to take out a form of credit, like a clothing account or credit card, to boost your credit score; however, make sure you pay your credit card on a monthly basis, too.

7. Business Credit Cards

If you need access to quick cash, getting a business credit card may be a good option for you. It works in the same way as a personal credit card where the lender gives you a card with a credit limit. You are then expected to make monthly repayments with interest. The more consistent you are at paying your business credit card, the more your credit limit will increase which will give you access to more cash. However, just like personal credit cards, the interest charged on credit cards is among the highest. Therefore, you should avoid using your credit card as though it was your petty cash; instead, only use it for financial emergencies.

LOANS FOR FOOD TRUCKS

Another option when it comes to business financing is to apply for a business loan. Typically, business loans are useful when you need to borrow a large sum of money to purchase expensive items like the food truck or kitchen equipment. Below is a list of food truck loans that you can consider:

1. Traditional Bank Loan

When seeking loans, you can first approach your local bank. Banks tend to offer reasonable interest rates on a variety of business loans (in your case, you would opt for a small business loan). Nonetheless, banks are known to enforce some of the strictest rules when it comes to approving loans. They will only consider applicants who are creditworthy and have an exceptional credit history. They may also expect you to have been in business for several years and have a consistent stream of revenue coming into your business before approving your loan application.

2. Small Business Administration (SBA) Loans

SBA-approved loans are great for food truck businesses who have been unsuccessful in obtaining a bank loan. The SBA covers a portion of the loan amount in the event that the business fails, or the owner fails to meet monthly repayments. However, your credit profile still applies when seeking approval for this type of loan; applicants are expected to have a credit score of 650 or higher. When the SBA-loan is approved, it can be used to purchase a vehicle; food supplies and equipment; or used as working capital.

3. Merchant Cash Advances

While these aren't exactly considered loans, merchant cash advances work in a similar way. They are a business-to-business financing solution that offers food truck owners cash up front for a percentage of the business's bank deposits or credit card transactions. This should ideally be the last option you consider, as merchant cash advances have the highest interest rates (apart from credit cards). However, since they don't require food truck owners to have a good credit profile, many owners may be drawn toward them. Repayments on merchant cash advances are automated and are made at the end of each business day.

4. Crowdfunding

Another creative way to raise funds for your start-up business is through crowdfunding. Crowdfunding platforms like GoFundMe and Kickstarter offer debt-free financing where a community of generous consumers, entrepreneurs, activists, and creatives donate funds toward small businesses that appeal to their interests. As the business receives the funds, you are not expected to pay it back—even if your food truck business fails. This may be a great alternative if you don't meet the requirements to apply for a loan. The only investment you will need to make is your time and strengthening your marketing efforts so that more people get to support your crowdfunding initiative.

CHAPTER 5
HOW TO FIND THE RIGHT TRUCK

A food truck is a large expense, but thankfully, there are a few ways of reducing your initial costs when purchasing a truck. For instance, if you cannot afford to buy a brand new truck, you can lease one or purchase a used vehicle. Before you decide on which strategy is best for you, you will need to weigh the pros and cons of each option.

OPTION 1: PURCHASING A NEW FOOD TRUCK

Think of purchasing a new food truck as a big investment decision you are undertaking. Like any investment, it can prove profitable, or it can backfire. Start-up entrepreneurs who have no prior experience in the food truck industry are advised to move away from this option. Even if you can afford to buy a new truck, you are better off investing that cash in other areas of your business. Purchasing a new food truck works well if you already understand the business climate; have seen the market ebb and flow; and have existing revenue coming into your business every month.

In most cases, food truck owners who purchase new vehicles are those who have successfully established their brand and are ready to take their business to greater heights. They are also likely to be owners planning on keeping their food truck for the next 5–10 years. Thus, if you are a food truck owner still testing out your food truck concept, it's better to go for the leasing option, as it comes with less risks.

Besides the cost of the truck, another factor you will need to consider when purchasing a new vehicle is its size. Determining the size of the vehicle you want will help you buy the appropriate kitchen equipment to fit inside your truck, as well as to plan a menu according to the space you will have in your truck. Before purchasing the vehicle, research your city's rules and restrictions about food truck sizes.

Once you know what size your vehicle ought to be, you will need to decide on buying an outfitted or custom-built food truck. The majority of food trucks on sale in the market are sold with fitted mobile kitchens—some even come with fitted kitchen equipment and sanitation systems (like enclosed toilets). Nonetheless, there are also basic trucks that don't come with fitted kitchens which are a lot more affordable compared to outfitted trucks. The only downside to buying a basic truck is that you will need to spend more money paying a manufacturer to install a mobile kitchen for you. If money isn't an issue, and perhaps you desire a custom truck that represents your unique brand, you can find a manufacturer with experience customizing food trucks that meet the health department's health and safety guidelines.

The benefits of purchasing a new truck is that you don't need to worry about vehicle breakdowns or unexpected costly repairs. Your new truck will likely come with a service plan and a warranty, protecting you from any manufacturing faults and saving you money on routine services. Moreover, if you decide to customize your truck, you can create a visual masterpiece that catches the attention of pedestrians wherever you go! The major drawback of purchasing a new truck is the expense involved. There's no getting around how expensive new trucks can be. Thus, buying a brand new vehicle may not be the most financially savvy decision for start-up businesses.

OPTION 2: LEASING A FOOD TRUCK

While purchasing a new food truck is more affordable than purchasing a brick-and-mortar restaurant, leasing a food truck offers far more flexibility than purchasing one straight from a dealership. Flexibility is a keyword for start-up businesses that already face multiple risks and challenges. Having the ability to end a lease or switch to a more affordable lease agreement can help start-up entrepreneurs manage their finances within the first few years.

Leasing a food truck is often seen as a short-term strategy designed for foodpreneurs who want to try out a new business concept or sample a menu. It protects their financial interests by taking away the need to invest a lump sum of capital up front or take out a business loan with high interest. Rental costs differ depending on the service provider; model and features of the vehicle; as well as the length of the lease. For example, if you commit to a lease of six months or more, you can expect to pay around $2,000 to $3,000 rent per month. Some rental fees include commissary costs, and others don't. Read through your contract carefully before you sign on the dotted line.

Leasing a food truck on a short-term basis can be a little more expensive than leasing it for an extended period of time. This is because the shorter the lease, the less turnover the service provider makes. It's common for food truck businesses to lease their trucks for one to two years or until they become successful and can afford to buy a new food truck. Nowadays, with the rising cost of living and the high costs that come with maintaining a vehicle, many successful food truck owners are choosing to remain renters.

Before renting a food truck, do your research, visit a number of service providers, and find out if you or your service provider will be responsible for paying vehicle insurance, maintenance fees, permits and licenses, commissary kitchen rental, parking, and so on. Also, find out what other benefits your lease comes with that can help you save costs on your business. Pay close attention to lease expiration dates and have a plan for when your lease is up. Look into renewal possibilities and lease-to-purchase options at the very beginning.

OPTION 3: PURCHASING A USED FOOD TRUCK

If you decide to get a food truck, you have two options: purchasing a new or used vehicle. Once again, it's essential to examine the benefits and drawbacks of each option before you commit to one. We have already spoken about the ins and outs of purchasing a new truck, so now, we will discuss the option of purchasing a used truck. The obvious benefit of buying a used vehicle is that it's more affordable than buying a new or custom vehicle. Even though your choices are limited, you are able to choose a truck in the best possible shape, lowest mileage, and with little to no vehicle faults.

This option is suitable for start-up businesses that are committed to the food truck business for the long haul but don't have a large pool of money to invest up front. But with any investment comes risks, and the risks of getting a used vehicle is that it could require expensive repairs jobs that defeat the purpose of saving money. Therefore, when you are searching for a used vehicle, make sure that you ask salesmen for the paperwork of the vehicle history that indicates its current condition. It's better to know from the onset what issues the vehicle comes with. If you can, get a mechanic to test-drive and assess the condition of the used food truck before you make your purchase.

The good news is that you can most likely negotiate the price of a used food truck, especially if you are buying the vehicle directly from the initial owner. You can find food truck listings on multiple listing platforms online, such as Craigslist, eBay, or Facebook Marketplace. If you have a food truck association in your area, you may find that they have their own market-place where food truck owners can sell their vehicles or equipment.

How can you assess when a used food truck is in good condition? Simple. You can conduct the following checks and balances:

1. Look at the engine and truck equipment: Engine and equipment repairs can be costly, so sometimes, the only solution is to buy a new engine or new equipment. If you are not qualified to assess the condition of an engine, get a mechanic to assess it for you. You can also get an appliance specialist to test the appliances in the truck.

2. Look over the truck's maintenance history: Verify the maintenance work done to the truck by looking over the maintenance records. These records will show you how many times the truck was serviced, what major repairs it had done, and any vehicle damages it has accumulated over the years.

3. Review the vehicle manufacturer: You may not be familiar with the model and make of the truck you want to purchase. Do a quick Google search to find out more about the manufacturer and what other people are saying about their fleet of cars. Look at customer reviews and ratings to get an idea of your experience as one of their vehicle holders.

4. Consider the age of the truck: In general, the older the truck, the more affordable it is, but purchasing a vehicle older than five years can expose you to many more risks. If you insist on getting a really old model (perhaps it's part of the design and brand look you are going for), make sure it has been maintained fairly well over the years.

5. Consider the mileage on the truck: Similar to the previous point, the higher the mileage of a vehicle, the more affordable it is. However, high mileage means a lot more maintenance work in the pipelines. If you cannot get a used vehicle with a low mileage, ask the salesman about the warranty on the vehicle. If you are given a warranty (or at least offered to extend the vehicle's warranty) you won't have to worry about any future maintenance work needed on your truck.

CHAPTER 6
FOOD TRUCK
EQUIPMENT CHECKLIST

A fter purchasing your food truck, there's only one more thing to do before you can start cooking: organize a list of food truck equipment. As mentioned before, you don't have to purchase brand new equipment. You can lease your equipment until you have committed to a specific menu. Nevertheless, you must ensure that you have the necessary tools and equipment to prepare a variety of meals, so you aren't limited to what you can serve customers.

FOOD PREPARATION EQUIPMENT

These tools, gadgets, and utensils are the most used in your food truck. They cover all of the supplies you will need to help you put together mouthwatering meals. While some food preparation supplies are standard, there will be other tools or gadgets that are necessary for the kinds of foods you will be serving. Here is a checklist to start you off:

- Stainless steel prep counter
- Cutting board
- Chef's knives
- Frying pans or skillets
- Sauce pans
- Thermometer
- Food processor or blender
- Turner
- French fry cutter

WARMING AND HOLDING EQUIPMENT

Warming and holding equipment ensures that your food remains at room temperature while you prepare other meals that are included in the order. Food warmers also help you keep your ready-meals safe from foodborne illnesses. To warm and hold your food, you will need to have at least four pieces of equipment:

- Countertop food warmer
- Fry dump station (keeps your fries warm after coming out of the fryer)
- Soup warmer
- Kettle or flask

COOKING EQUIPMENT

The main kitchen equipment you will need is cooking equipment. These will be the machines that grill, fry, bake, steam, or toast your food. It's important to wait until you have your food truck floor plan before buying or leasing cooking equipment so that you make sure you have enough space in your truck to fit your cooking equipment. Here is a checklist of standard cooking equipment:

- Flat-top grill or griddle
- Cooking range
- Microwave
- Toaster
- Charbroiler
- Cheese melter
- Deep fryer
- Food truck exhaust hood

REFRIGERATION EQUIPMENT

Refrigeration equipment is another necessity for your food truck. They keep your ingredients chilled so that they stay fresher for longer. At the very least, you will need one refrigerator fitted in your mobile kitchen, but if you have enough space, you can have a variety of refrigerators to chill or prepare different foods. Here is a list of your options:

- Under-counter or worktop refrigerator
- Pizza preparation refrigerator
- Sandwich and salad preparation refrigerator
- Under-counter freezers

FOOD TRUCK SUPPLIES

Since food trucks sell food on the go, you will need to have plenty of disposable serving supplies. Make sure that you have enough storage in your truck to neatly pack away your supplies. Moreover, ensure that at the beginning of each day, you have sufficient supplies to cover all of your meals. For instance, running out of disposable utensils could mean having to close up shop. Here is a checklist of some of the food supplies you will need:

- Serving utensils
- Condiment dispenser
- Squeeze bottles (to allow customers to pour their own sauces)
- Spice shakers
- Paper food trays
- Plastic or foam dinnerware
- Plastic or foam cups
- Plastic eating utensils
- Takeout containers
- Paper napkins and dispenser

- Guest order forms
- Aluminum or plastic food wrap
- Disposable gloves

JANITORIAL EQUIPMENT

The U.S. Department of Health sets high standards for cleanliness when it comes to food truck businesses. Thus, having cleaning supplies is necessary to maintain a sanitary environment on your truck. Here is a list of some of the janitorial supplies you will need:

- A built-in sink (preferably with three compartments for washing, rinsing, and sanitizing dishes)
- A small hand sink where employees can wash their hands or rinse food ingredients
- Wet area floor mats to prevent slipping
- Sanitizing liquid to clean hands, wipe counters, etc.
- Scrubbing brushes and sponges
- Trash can and disposable liners
- Mop and bucket
- Broom and dustpan

CHAPTER 7
WHAT'S ON THE MENU?

F ood truck chefs have brought a new sense of magic in how traditional meals are prepared. You may have eaten a burger before, but have you ever had a barbecue shredded pork burger with Luciano's secret sauce? While food truck owners compete on several fronts, like finding the most ideal locations or creating the most appealing brands, when it comes to creating a mouthwatering menu, nearly all food trucks reign supreme. There are just so many different ways of reinventing popular foods that each food truck has the freedom to sample their own recipes and create what will be their signature dishes. What's more, customers enjoy testing out new foods, so they won't mind you switching up the menu every once in a while!

If I were to describe food truck menus in a phrase, it would be, "Gourmet food on a budget." Don't mistake their affordable prices for serving low-quality food. There's almost an unspoken rule in the food truck industry that every meal served must be similar or better than restaurant food. The reason food truck menus are more affordable than restaurant menus is because you are paying for the product and its prepa- ration—not for a waitress to take your order or for the water and electricity bill of the establishment. Moreover, food truck owners reinvest every penny saved on costs to produce more exotic meals that push the boundaries of innovation.

HOW TO CREATE A MENU CONCEPT FOR A FOOD TRUCK BUSINESS

As a food truck owner, your goal is to ensure that your menu makes your food truck the talk of the town. Yes, creating a powerful brand and marketing your business will get you customers, but nothing is more convincing than customers sharing experiences with their friends of your delicious food. Humans perceive the world through their five senses: sight, hearing, taste, smell, and touch. Ideally, your menu and food items should appeal to all five senses. As you go about creating your menu concept, remember the five senses at the back of your mind. Here are four other things to consider:

1. Be Clear on the Type of Food You Want to Serve

It's impossible to offer customers every type of cuisine. Even the best traditional restaurants focus on a particular niche and excel in it. When deciding on a cuisine, first consider what types of foods you enjoy preparing. Do you love making creamy pastas? Are you known as the barbecue champion among your circle of friends? Cooking foods you already have skill and knowledge about will automatically give you a competitive advantage. You can narrow your niche even further by selecting one or two specific meals from the broader cuisine that you would like to prepare. Doing this will also help you save costs on ingredients and other tools and equipment.

2. Consider Offering Seasonal Specials by Adding Your Unique Twist

Having seasonal specials on your menu is a great way to keep customers visiting your truck throughout the year. It also adds variation to your menu while ensuring that your signature dishes remain your highest grossing products. Ensure that you add your own creative flare in reinventing seasonal favorites, so you can stand out from the competition. This doesn't mean that you must completely change the recipe or add more ingredients. Your twist can be as simple as adding a secret ingredient that takes a classic from predictable to one of a kind!

3. Have Fun With Your Product Names

If you plan on starting a food truck selling waffles, I can guarantee you that every customer you serve has tried waffles before. However, I can also guarantee you that none of them have ever had Oreo Brownie Waffles before. Do you know why? Well, because it's a product name I've invented from the top of my head! Your menu can seem exotic by simply playing around with product names, and instead of listing items, you can describe them in the most creative ways. Along with the product names, you can show customers product photos, so they are able to visualize what some of these unique products look like.

4. Get Creative With Your Drinks, Too

It's common for both restaurant and food truck owners to put the least amount of effort in their drinks menu. This can be an opportunity lost, especially in the food truck business where customers are looking for items on the go. You never know when you might get a customer who's thirsty and only wants to try out your drinks. Consider the type of beverages customers want. In the mornings and on cold winter days, exotic coffee or tea beverages may be in high demand. If you are planning on visiting festivals or farmers' markets, you might find a lot of customers who are looking for virgin or alcoholic cocktails to enjoy with their meals. Make sure that you have a selection of drinks on offer, and don't be afraid to recreate traditional drinks, too!

THE MOST POPULAR FOOD TRUCK MENU CONCEPTS

Another way to create a menu concept for your food truck is to consider the target market your food truck will be catering to. Study your market's food preferences, eating habits, and the kinds of food trends they follow. For example, if you are targeting a market that is health-conscious, selling deep-fried chicken won't get you many customers. Instead, having low-fat, gluten-free, or vegan options might! Moreover, if you are catering to a market that enjoys fine dining and has a sophisticated palette, you will serve completely different food from a food truck catering to a market that enjoys fast food or casual street food.

If you still find it difficult to come up with your unique menu concept, you can adopt one of the popular food truck menu concepts. Even though food trucks have been around for many decades, only a few types of food trucks have been able to gain the public's vote. For example, hot dog carts are a classic example of a menu concept that works and won't go out of style anytime soon. You could adopt the popular hot dog cart concept, but make a few creative changes to your menu so that you remain competitive. Here are a few more popular food truck menu concepts that appeal to the masses:

1. Barbecue

There are some who love to cook over fire and others who enjoy eating grilled foods. There is something undeniably magical about food that's been prepared on an open flame. Whether the food is grilled or smoked, the flavors are more intense, and the experience becomes memorable. Barbecue requires less ingredients and equipment to prepare, making it a low-cost option. Add in your secret marinades and techniques to make your barbecue the best in the city. Here are a few common barbecue menu items you can reinvent:

- Brisket
- Mac and cheese
- Chicken wings
- Burgers
- Shish kebabs
- Barbecue seafood
- Pork ribs

2. Gourmet Sandwiches

There are a million ways to prepare a sandwich, and that's why gourmet sandwiches and paninis will never go out of style. The best part about eating a gourmet sandwich is not necessarily the ingredients that are used but how the chef has created a meal by mixing up ingredients and pairing flavors that you wouldn't expect to go together. Creating sandwiches also doesn't require much capital. You can base your sandwiches on seasonal ingredients and give your customers something to always look forward to with each season. Moreover, you can allow your customers to customize their own sandwiches, combining some of the ingredients they love. Here are a few food truck sandwich ideas:

- Nacho grilled cheese sandwiches
- Chicken Caesar wraps
- Pulled pork paninis
- Buttermilk fried chicken sandwiches
- Breakfast club sandwiches
- Savory waffle sandwiches

3. Desserts

Dessert trucks are gaining popularity and offering more variety than traditional ice cream trucks. They appeal to customers of all ages and usually make a great lunch option for those who aren't looking for savory foods. The success of a dessert menu depends on how well it can fulfill a customer's wildest dessert dreams! When opting for this type of menu, don't play it safe. Think big, go extreme, and have fun creating new twists on classic desserts. Here are a few dessert ideas to activate your creative brain:

- Gourmet donuts
- Ice cream tacos
- Crêpes
- Churros
- Ice cream sandwiches
- Mini dessert pies

- Smoothie bowls
- Gourmet popcorn

CREATING AN ATTRACTIVE FOOD TRUCK MENU BOARD

When you have decided on a menu and come up with creative product names, you will need to create a menu board to display your products to potential customers. Many food truck owners underestimate the importance of a menu board, and as a result, they either don't create one or scribble items on a chalkboard. As a result, these owners miss out on the opportunity of winning customers over by simply displaying food items in an aesthetically pleasing way. Taking time to plan your board and being intentional about how you organize your products can be free press for your business! Here are eight tips for designing your food truck menu board:

1. Make Sure Your Signature Meals Stand Out

All of your meals will have customers licking their plates, but only a few meals will have them coming back to your food truck. Your signature meals are those that make your business memorable and have customers spreading the word about your truck. These meals should be given the prime spots on your menu board, so that, even if a customer only samples your food once, at least they get to sample one of your signature meals! In general, the upper right-hand corner or center of your menu board are two great places to display your signature dishes. You can even think about writing them in a different font style, font size, or color so that passersby can quickly take notice of them.

2. Think of Creative Display Ideas

We have all seen the black chalkboard menu, and quite frankly, it has become predictable! Consider other ways of displaying your food menu that are distinct to your brand. For example, if you have decided on a barbecue menu, your menu board could be a custom chopping board with food items written on it. If you are serving a variety of ice cream dishes, you could have your menu displayed on a giant cone. There are no limits when it comes to thinking about innovative ways of selling your menu to potential customers.

3. Keep Your Menu Simple

You don't need to display every small food item you have to offer. Besides your signature dishes, you can include some of your best-selling side dishes and best-selling drinks. Remember: Your customer is looking for food on the go. They don't want to stand near your truck for hours looking through a list of options. Make their purchasing decision easier by offering fewer options on your menu. If they ask for something that is not on the menu (but related to what you offer), you can prepare a special order.

4. Make Sure Your Board Can Be Updated Frequently

As innovative as your board can be, it must also serve a practical purpose. Every now and again, your food prices will fluctuate, and you will need to update your board. Ensure that the materials you use for your board allow you to make customizations. For example, instead of engraving product names on your board, consider using a quality marker that can be wiped off whenever you need to update your board.

5. Choose the Appropriate Fonts and Colors

Treat your menu board like one of the marketing tools of your business. Ensure that it reinforces what your food truck is about and makes your business stand out from the rest. When using fonts and colors, maintain consistency with the other visual elements you have already used to sell your brand. This makes your brand cohesive and professional. You should also consider using fonts and colors that appeal to your audience. Think about how easy your font is to read and what your colors symbolize. Lastly, if you are considering adding product photos to your menu board, ensure that you take professional product photos that have been taken with a good camera.

6. Proofread Your Menu

There's nothing that says, "rushed job" like finding spelling mistakes on a menu board. Some might think an error like this is harmless but not when your reputation is on the line. Nowadays, customers expect a lot from businesses, especially those in the food industry who they trust to deliver quality meals. Finding mishaps on the menu board could reflect poorly on the business and cause customers to have doubts about the business's attention to detail. Build your credibility by proofreading your menu and making it have no errors.

7. Understand Menu Psychology

Retail stores plan their store layouts in a manner that encourages consumers to make a sale. This is known as retail psychology. As a food truck owner, the best way you can encourage customers to buy food from your truck is by understanding menu psychology. What you display on your menu, and how you display it, can positively influence customers to make a sale. For example, when designing your menu board, avoid writing dollar signs next to the cost of each meal. Doing so makes a customer focus more on the price of a product rather than the meal. Another tip is to add quirky adjectives in your product descriptions that cause potential customers to laugh, pay attention, or better yet... take a photo!

8. Ask For Feedback on Your Menu

Before publicly displaying your menu board for everyone to view, get a few close friends and family to look at it and give their honest feedback. Ask them to pretend as though they were customers and to share their first impressions about the menu and design of the menu board. The point here is to get an outsider's perspective on your board so that you can review potential blind spots you have missed. If you need to go back and make changes, give yourself enough time to do so.

Are you still contemplating what style of board to use on your food truck? Here are a few options that you can choose from, but remember to add your own creative flare to take your board up a notch:

Whiteboard menu: You've probably seen whiteboards in a school or office environment, but these flexible boards can also look great as a food menu display. Whiteboards are also easy to manage and clean, making them a good option when you want to trial several different menus. Make your menu stand out by making product descriptions short, increasing the font of prices, and including your brand's logo on the signage.

Chalkboard menu: This is one of the most popular menu board choices for food truck owners. It has a timeless look that presents menu items in an attractive way. They can also come in different sizes, making them an affordable option for start-up businesses. Similar to whiteboards, you can easily erase or make updates to your menu (although if you want special calligraphy used, you may need to hire a professional each time you want to add or remove something from your menu).

Custom laminated menu: If you are planning on having a large display menu that won't change often, you can get a laminated poster that you can pin up on the side of your truck. You can design your menu on an online graphic design software, like Canva, or have a professional graphic designer create one for you. Thereafter, you can visit your local printer store and get it laminated on the material of your choice. Laminated menus are a low-cost option that is also easy to clean. The only drawback is that it's semi-permanent, and any spelling or spacing errors made on the menu cannot be fixed without starting the lamination process from scratch.

Metal and hardboard menu: These boards are sleek sheets of metal that are bent and displayed on the exterior of your truck. They are solid and bold which helps customers move their eyes swiftly across the entire menu. Since metal boards are customizable, they can come with magnetic menu item slots and cards that are used to display different meals at different hourly or daily options. Nevertheless, a customized board like this can be costly, especially if you plan on hiring labor to install it on the side of your truck.

Butcher paper roll menu: As visually appealing and creative as it is, this option is perhaps the most affordable, costing you less than $10. Large pieces of butcher paper roll can be used as material to display your menu. It can give your truck a rugged or rustic feel, which is perfect if your brand has a similar feel. Even though you can't erase content from your butcher paper roll, you can easily replace it with another long piece of paper. The only possible drawback is that you will need to have a lot of paper roll on hand and get a professional calligrapher to design your menu on it whenever you need a redo.

High-definition TV display menu: If you are a fan of tech gadgets, why not display your menu on a high-definition TV screen? This way, you don't need to hire professionals to handwrite your menu or worry about replacing your board when it suffers wear and tear. You can connect your TV screen to a computer in the truck, and paste slides of the menu for customers to look at. If you're really tech savvy, you can even add a video element or music to enhance the viewing experience.

Truck wrap menu: The final option is to have your menu wrapped on the side of your truck. Once again, there is no need to have a physical board or worry about replacing your board every so often. Plus, wherever you drive your truck, you are guaranteed to have people eyeing your menu and knowing what you offer. As attractive as this option is, it is a permanent feature that remains on your truck until you decide to change the wrapping. Make sure you are 100% sold on the idea and willing to live with it for 5–10 years before deciding to continue.

STRATEGIES FOR GETTING THE BEST PRICING FOR YOUR MENU

A perfect food truck menu is also one that is priced right. What is the right price for your meals? Well, the price you set is determined by the time and money you invest in buying, preparing, and delivering delicious meals. Of course, the less money you spend in the process of producing your meals, the more affordable they will be. It's tempting as a new food truck owner to enter the market with the lowest meal prices. After all, you significantly under cut your competitor's prices and potentially gain more customers. The truth, however, is that opting for the lowest price is not always a good business move, since your aim is to at least reach your break-even point every month. Pricing too low or pricing too high can put substantial strain on your business. Keeping this in mind, here are a few strategies to help you determine the best pricing for your menu:

1. Consider the List of Food Costs

Before you can determine a price for a meal, you need to make a list of all the food ingredients you will need to make it and how much they will cost you. Don't forget to add smaller ingredients like spices or ketchup. Calculate the food ingredients you will need per portion size to get the most accurate food costs; this means you will need to work out the cost per serving for each food ingredient. Account for factors like fluctuating food prices or the cost difference when certain foods are not in season.

2. Consider the Ongoing Market Rate

The cost of your meals should be set to what customers are relatively comfortable paying for and what similar food trucks are charging. This is known as the market rate. Setting high prices for foods that have a relatively low market rate can push customers away. The only way you can get away with setting high prices is if you can communicate that your meals include high-quality ingredients that are difficult to source or worth every penny. Setting low prices isn't a bad strategy, either. A low price doesn't communicate low quality; instead low prices appeal to price-conscious customers who are looking for affordable alternatives.

3. Consider the Inventory You Carry

It's common among food truck owners to set food prices based on the inventory of food they carry. This can offer owners flexibility in adjusting food prices when certain ingredients become harder to source. It also allows owners to base their prices on the amount of money they have already spent on stocking ingredients and takes into account losses due to food wastage or spoilage.

4. Consider the Time You Invest in Preparing Food

Food truck owners, especially if they are also the chef in charge, often forget to factor in the time spent preparing meals when calculating meal prices. Calculating time spent preparing food isn't as tailored as calculating cost of food items. If you are starting out and you already have a stable job on the side, you may not need to factor your time in the meal price. However, if cooking for your truck is going to be your main source of income, then you will need to factor labor costs when calculating your meal prices.

5. Consider Overhead Costs per Meal

Lastly, overheads are another factor that you can consider when pricing your menu. Each meal may have its own variable costs (the expenses involved in producing the meal), but above and beyond the variable costs, you will need to consider other overheads like taxes, gas, parking fees, marketing, and insurance. When calculating your daily overhead costs, divide your costs by the number of people you plan on serving on a daily basis.

CHAPTER 8
PREPARING FOOD—THE WHERE'S AND HOW'S

Sourcing food has a significant impact on the success of your food truck business. For example, sourcing food from expensive supplies will increase the cost of producing your meals and eat away at your potential profits. Moreover, ordering the incorrect volume of food can also cut back your profits and limit the number of people you are able to serve a day. The best tip when it comes to sourcing is to plan ahead of time, so you can compare different food prices and receive your orders in due time. Start planning by making detailed food lists, writing down the quantity of food you need, and seeing how much you are able to store away while keeping the food fresh. It's always better to order less quantity of food than to have a lot of food that you can't sell because it has gone bad.

BEST PLACES TO SOURCE YOUR FOOD

Ideally, it is a lot easier to source your food locally because it requires less planning and organization. Local ingredients can even be fresher and give your business a great marketing angle, as consumers love businesses that support local economies. However, your local suppliers may not always give you the best deals on food. As a start-up business, you are looking for quality ingredients at the most affordable price, and sometimes, this means sourcing food from other cities, towns, or states. A large shipment carrying food from a large supplier can offer better rates on food, especially when you purchase some items in bulk. With this said, you should consider several suppliers and weigh the cost of sourcing locally or out of town. Here are a few sources to consider:

1. Wholesale Food Distributors

There are many wholesale food distributors that you can find online through sites like Foodservice.com which offer directories of food and beverage suppliers. You can also search for food wholesalers around your area or approach the major ones like Sysco or US Foods.

2. Food Manufacturers

Food manufacturers can either sell you what you need or point you to major food stores or wholesalers they supply with products. You can start your search online by looking for manufacturers nearby or in your city. A quick search will pull up thousands of manufacturers to consider—even smaller manufacturers that focus on producing niche products. For example, you can find manufacturers whose main product is tacos or fries. Since there is no shortage of manufacturers, compare the prices of several of them before settling on one.

3. Local Food Distributors

If you want to save yourself the hassle of sourcing different foods from different manufacturers, you can simply approach a local food distributor that stocks a variety of food products from various wholesalers and manufacturers. The only drawback with this option is that you may pay more for goods since you aren't sourcing them directly from the supplier. However, the advantage is that they are local and can handle most of the logistics involved in sourcing the food.

4. Greenmarkets and Farmers' Markets

An alternative method for sourcing fresh local ingredients is to visit farmers' markets. Fresh foods sold at markets are usually produced by small-scale farmers who live on the outskirts of the city. By supporting local farmers, you can boost your local agricultural industry and ensure that there are more producers of organic ingredients. You can get to know farmers by visiting greenmarkets or farmers' markets and learning more about how their products are grown and stored.

5. Food Cooperatives

When food truck owners come together and order food in bulk, sharing the costs involved, they can save a lot of money. Of course, this only works when each food truck owner specializes in noncompetitive menus. The larger the order that is placed, the higher the discounts. This is how a food cooperative is formed. To create your own food co-op, look for local food trucks or restaurants that don't sell similar foods as you. Speak to the owners and find out if they would like to join your co-op. The more individuals you can get to join, the more money each of you will save when buying food. If you can't find anyone to join your co-op, you can research local co-ops and join an existing group.

6. Shopping Clubs

Another modern way of sourcing food is by joining a shopping club like Sam's Club or BJ's Wholesale Club. Shopping clubs give members the opportunity to buy quality products in bulk. All types of food businesses join shopping clubs, so you will most likely source your food from the same place as many restaurants and food trucks. To join, you would need to sign up for a membership and pay an annual fee.

FOOD SAFETY TIPS FOR YOUR FOOD TRUCK BUSINESS

With more and more consumers making food trucks their first choice for on-the-go meals, it has become necessary for food

truck owners to manage the health and safety of their operations. American consumers are a lot more knowledgeable
about food than they were a few decades ago. As a result, they
are curious to know where their food is sourced, how it is
prepared, and whether the people preparing their food follow
the necessary health guidelines.

Food truck businesses must prove to the general public that
their food is just as fresh as restaurant food. They need to
show customers that despite having less space to prepare food,
they abide by the health and safety protocols set out by the
health department. One of the reasons many food trucks are
forced to shut down is due to receiving poor health assess-
ments. According to data from the Los Angeles County
Department of Public Health, 27% of food trucks in the city
received a grade lower than an A after health inspections were
conducted (Sheetz, 2020). This shows how much of a challenge it is for food trucks to maintain health and hygiene
standards.

Health officials have seen it all when it comes to unsatisfac-
tory health measures followed by food trucks, from dirty utensils and dishes piling up on countertops to rodent infestation
and droppings found in trucks. Common health risks associated with outside pests include improper refrigeration,
improper hand washing procedures, cross-contamination of
foods, and inadequately sanitized surfaces. These risks can

compromise the freshness and quality of foods, making them unsafe to eat.

Maintaining cleanliness in a small food truck may be difficult, but it isn't impossible. By following the tips below, you can minimize the potential risk of foodborne illnesses in your truck:

1. Wash your hands regularly: Dirty hands are the fastest spreaders of foodborne illnesses. Get in the habit of washing your hands before and after you handle different foods to ensure the highest hygiene standards.

2. Put proper measures in place to store refrigerated foods: To reduce bacterial growth, ensure that you store refrigerated foods at a temperature of 40 °F or lower. If you notice that your refrigerating system is faulty and isn't reaching the proper temperatures, store your food in cooler boxes filled with ice. Pay attention to the expiry dates on your refrigerated foods to ensure proper management.

3. Sanitize all food preparation stations or surfaces: To avoid cross contamination, ensure that you properly clean and sanitize your utensils; pots and pans; and countertops. Once a week, clean and sanitize your kitchen cooking equipment, like your microwave, oven, fryer, and grill.

4. Keep a thermometer in the truck: Every food truck should have a reliable thermometer in the truck to ensure that food is cooked thoroughly, and all harmful bacteria has been eliminated. If you are going to have kitchen staff, make sure they are familiar with the various internal temperatures for foods.

5. Wash all of your produce before you start cooking them: A common food-related disease that consumers have contracted from food trucks is food poisoning. Food poisoning can be due to cross contamination of raw and cooked foods or dirty produce. Even food that looks clean can have dirt on it, so it's important to hand-wash produce regardless of how clean it may look.

DOES YOUR BUSINESS NEED A COMMISSARY KITCHEN?

Many food trucks are turning to commissary kitchens to assist them in preparing their meals. There are a few reasons for this, like the lack of preparation space, the inability to handle large volumes inside the truck, and the need to reduce food waste and ensure that health and safety standards are adhered to. Commissary kitchens are commercial kitchens where food businesses can go to prepare and store their food. There are some commissary kitchens that cater specifically to food trucks, but for the most part, even traditional restaurants and catering businesses are able to rent space at a commissary kitchen.

There are a few commissary kitchens that you can choose from depending on your needs and budget:

Shared commercial kitchen: This is the most economical option for start-up food truck businesses looking for preparation space. Several chefs and food service providers share cooking and storage facilities and are given designated time slots when they can utilize the kitchen.

Private commercial kitchen: If you have the budget, you can rent out a private kitchen where you have more space and time to cook. Instead of splitting the cost of rent with other food business owners, you would cover the entire lease on your own. This option works well for established food truck businesses owning multiple food trucks and looking for a central hub where they can prepare food and store ingredients.

Renting a restaurant's kitchen: Another option is to rent out a restaurant's kitchen during their off hours. It's similar to renting a private commercial kitchen, but the cost is significantly less. The only drawback may be the lack of cooking amenities and storage or parking space at your chosen restaurant.

Nontraditional commercial kitchens: There are other public spaces that offer kitchens that you can use (sometimes at no cost at all). For example, if you are a member of a local church, you can ask to use their kitchen, provided they are commercial kitchens and have the correct commercial-grade equipment. Other public spaces include schools, retirement villages, or social clubs.

According to some city or state laws, it is mandatory that food truck businesses use commissary kitchens. To find out if this law applies to your business, you will need to reach out to local officials and ask for guidance.

CHAPTER 9
CHOOSING A LOCATION

Purchased a truck?

Check!

Got the proper kitchen gear?

Of course!

And what about a show-stopping menu?

Yes, I have that, too!

Since the main elements of your business have been discussed, the rest of the chapters in this book will explore other factors that can multiply the success of your food truck. In other words, what you have learned up until now will get you started in legalizing, financing, and getting your food truck started. However, what you are about to learn in the next few chapters will ensure that your truck survives through the first year and becomes a mega success in your city!

One of the main selling points of starting a food truck business is that it offers foodpreneurs more flexibility. Unlike a brick-and-mortar restaurant that is fixed in one location, a food truck can travel to several different locations across the city, searching for its ideal customers. Instead of waiting on customers to find you, you can get out there and search for them. Picking the best location for your food truck can multiply the success of your business and give it the exposure it deserves. But finding the best location isn't as easy as putting gas into your truck and parking in random spots across town. There are a lot of factors to consider when choosing a location where you are guaranteed long lines and lots of happy customers!

FINDING THE PERFECT PARKING LOCATION FOR YOUR FOOD TRUCK

The food truck business and real estate investing are perhaps two businesses where location is critical to success. You could have the best food menu and unbeatable prices but are parked in a location with barely any foot traffic or interested consumers. It's always mentioned that food truck owners have a lot of freedom and flexibility in running their businesses, but how this freedom and flexibility is used matters, too.

A 2018 analysis by CARTO found that where food trucks parked across New York City influenced how much revenue they made per week. For example, the company found that the average food truck makes $11,000 in sales per week, but trucks parked in Corona Park, Queens brought in $6,128 per week, and trucks parked in the West Village brought in $5,234 per week (Miles, 2018). This shows that a distance of 10 miles between neighborhoods can make close to $1,000 difference in revenue. Consider the following things when looking for your ideal parking location:

1. Parking, Zoning, and Permit Requirements

Before making up your mind about a location, find out if food trucks are even allowed to park there. If they are, find out which permits and licenses you will apply for. Some cities and towns may also enforce parking restrictions on food trucks and limit the amount of hours you can remain parked in one space. Others ban food trucks from operating on the roads between certain times of the day. If you have applied for a permit or license, get your legal work approved before securing your parking location.

2. Look For Places With Foot Traffic

As a food truck owner, you make the most money in places that receive a lot of foot traffic. Drive around town and note several places where you see a lot of people either walking by, eating, or relaxing. For example, you can look for busy streets;

outdoor food courts or markets; or parks and other outdoor recreational facilities. However, you should remember that the more foot traffic a place has, the more competitors you will need to rival with. For example, downtown in any city receives a lot of foot traffic, but every other competing food truck knows that, too! If you are planning on appealing to crowds of people, prepare to compete with other established food truck brands and have the capacity to feed a lot of hungry customers!

3. Find the Best Schedule

You'll find it difficult to build a solid customer base when you change locations consistently. While it's acceptable within the first few weeks of running your food truck, you will need to eventually settle down and get into a predictable schedule. You can create your schedule by setting work hours for yourself and showing up at the same location during the same time of day. This will help customers plan their meals according to your truck's opening hours and anticipate your arrival.

4. Get Involved With Local Events

Partnering with local events is another way to get the news out about your food truck and find locations with a lot of foot traffic. When you park at a festival or a farmer's market, you are guaranteed customers, depending on the popularity of the event. Attending events like these can also give you an opportunity to test new menu items and get honest feedback about the quality of your food and your menu prices. When planning to attend a local event, get organized ahead of time. Consider parking fees, food costs, and ways to freshen up your menu. If you already have an established customer base, you can ask them to attend the event and show their support.

5. Increase Your Presence Online

Social media presence has become a fundamental aspect of many businesses, including food truck businesses. While a lot of people are able to interact with your food truck as they walk past, you can appeal to those who may live around the area but may not have walked or driven past your food truck before. Consider social networking sites, like Instagram or Pinterest, which allow you to capture images of your food and faces of happy customers. Encourage your customers to tag you whenever they post photos of your food. Engage with your followers and create an online group of ambassadors for your business.

BEST LOCATION IDEAS FOR YOUR FOOD TRUCK BUSINESS

Not every location is perfect for your type of food truck business. Depending on your particular brand, target market, and selection of foods and beverages, you will need to choose a location that matches your business model. Here are a few popular locations that appeal to various food truck businesses:

1. Festivals and Concerts

If your food truck appeals to a young and hip audience, you will fit right in at a festival or concert venue. Get acquainted with event organizers and stay up to date with events taking place throughout the city. On the week of the event, be on the lookout for bad weather, as it may cause the festival to be canceled which would cause you to lose a lot of money. It's also worth looking through the list of people who follow the festival's page on social media to see whether they fall under your target market. If not, you may not end up making a lot of sales at the event due to not offering the kinds of foods they eat.

2. Business Districts

Your food truck may appeal to the busy employee who can only afford to spend a few minutes out of the office. When serving food to professionals, you can offer several meals a day, like breakfast, lunch, and an afternoon snack to grab on the way home. Hungry employees are always snacking, so ensure that you have plenty of coffee and baked goods in the morning and small, bite-sized snacks during the day. It may also be good to have other employees helping you place preorders and serve meals throughout the day. The last thing you want is to make your customer miss a meeting or fall behind on their work tasks!

3. Street Parking

Street parking works well when you're targeting ordinary pedestrians passing by. Therefore, to find the best parking spot, look for streets with high foot traffic. You don't necessarily have to park on a main road to get the attention of people. Parking just off a busy street will work, plus it will help you avoid causing traffic with your truck. If you notice new construction taking place in your town, you can also park within close proximity to the construction site, so you can serve the workers breakfast and lunch meals.

4. Shopping Districts

Indoor shopping malls come with their own food courts and restaurants; however, smaller strip malls don't always have a variety of restaurants serving on-the-go food. These open plan shopping districts with outdoor areas can be great places to set up a food truck. Set up a meeting with the shopping district manager and find out the rules and regulations pertaining to food trucks. If you get the green light from the mall, pay a visit a few times to see the best time of day to serve customers. Selling food at a shopping district doesn't need to be your primary location; it can be a spot you visit at the end of each month (when malls are usually packed) or on weekends.

5. Farmers' Markets

What better place to park your food truck than in a location where people go to buy food? A farmer's market is an outdoor food market selling mostly organically grown produce and other homemade delicacies sold by small-scale food businesses. Nowadays, people visit farmers' markets not only to stock up on grocery supplies but to socialize and enjoy outdoor entertainment. It's common to find food truck stalls at farmers' markets selling all sorts of exotic foods and beverages. Similar to setting up at shopping districts, this option isn't typically the primary location for many food truck businesses but rather one they go to on weekends or certain times of the month.

6. College Campuses

If you ask college students what they think about the food they are served in their dining halls by outsourced catering companies, you'll hear a lot of bad reviews. Even those students who have their own kitchens prefer to eat out rather than cook fresh and delicious meals. A college campus can be a great primary spot for your truck if your brand is youthful and offers student-friendly meals. You can also earn more revenue if you set up from the morning and sell foods throughout the day until the evening. (Many students stay on campus until late hours of the night and may need to buy themselves dinner or snacks to keep them energized.)

7. Truck Parks

The concept of truck parks is relatively new in most parts of the U.S. Due to the increase in popularity of food trucks, truck

WALTER GRANT & ANDREW HUDSON

owners selling noncompetitive meals have decided to partner with each other and sell food in a single location. This strategy has been successful so far, as it has piqued the interest of consumers and given them more variety of foods to choose from. At the end of the day, even if one truck gets more business than another, all of them end up making higher revenue by leveraging their networks. Truck parks don't need to be open every day of the week. The group of truck owners can decide which days of the month suit them and for how many hours their stores will be opened. Planning in advance can also enable them to market their truck park on social media so that more crowds of people can visit and support the businesses.

8. Bars and Nightclubs

If you are working at a nine-to-five during the week and only have your weekends open, you can consider doubling your revenue by working night shifts near a local bar or nightclub. Of course, this option only works for night owls who don't mind working during night hours. When people leave bars and nightclubs, they often crave a quick meal that they can feast on at home. Since many fast-food stops or restaurants aren't open during these hours, they are more likely to buy from your truck if it is nearby. Moreover, if there is hardly any competition in that area, you could make a lot of money in just a few hours of work. You can draw customers to your truck by parking within close proximity to bars and nightclubs so that customers smell the aromas coming from your truck when they enter and leave the premises. It's also wise to be acquainted with bar or nightclub owners and try your best to be on good terms in order for your business relationship to remain profitable.

9. Gas Stations

Another unconventional location to park your food truck is at a local gas station. You can target customers who are going there to fill up their cars, use the public bathrooms, or stock up on food supplies. Many of the workers at the gas station, construction workers, and members of law enforcement may visit your truck during their lunch breaks. In general, gas station managers welcome food trucks because of the business they bring to the gas station which ends up creating a win-win scenario. However, there are some who may prohibit food trucks or enforce rules and regulations that food trucks must follow (such as what foods you can or can't sell or the times of day your business can operate).

CHAPTER 10
HIRING STAFF FOR YOUR FOOD TRUCK BUSINESS

There will come a time where the demand for your food will increase, and you will need employees to help you run your food truck business. When you reach this point, give yourself a pat on the back and pop a bottle of champagne to celebrate your business growth! Although once the champagne has been sipped, put your business hat back on and get your notebook out because you will need to prepare your hiring strategy. Hiring people for your food truck business isn't as easy as putting up an ad on Craigslist and hoping that at least one person responds. You must consider many factors like your budget for paying salaries, how many hours you will need your employees to work for, and what roles you would like them to fill. This chapter will give you an overview of things to consider when hiring staff and tips for recruiting the best team!

HOW TO DETERMINE YOUR FOOD TRUCK'S STAFFING NEEDS

When you are ready to recruit staff, your focus will be on finding the right people to fill positions in your business. But before you do that, I would like you to focus on your role as a leader. As soon as you hire anybody to work alongside you, you need to become a manager—someone responsible for training employees and making sure they have all of the resources, skills, and knowledge required for them to succeed. Not only do you need to train and manage your employees, you will also be responsible for sharing the business mission and objectives with them so that they are passionate about the business as much as you. I encourage you to read a few entrepreneurial and leadership books to prepare yourself for a lifelong role as a leader. Determine your own strengths and weaknesses, so you can find an ideal leadership style that works for your business and suits your personality.

Now that we've got that out of the way, the next thing to remember is to be patient when looking for the best employees. If you rush the hiring process, you might end up with employees who are only interested in the paycheck they will receive at the end of the month and not about your food truck. You need to find people who are genuinely passionate about your business and can relate to your brand. There will be times when you cannot interact with your customers, and one of your staff members will need to stand in your place and be the face of your food truck. Even though your employees may not be putting in long hours like you, make sure that they enjoy engaging with customers; speaking about or preparing food; and most importantly, working for you.

Next, you will need to determine your unique staffing needs. Unlike traditional restaurants, food trucks don't need to have a lot of employees. Since you are operating your food business on a truck, you are limited in terms of the number of individuals who can help you run your business. In general, food truck owners hire two or three employees who are qualified to handle a variety of tasks. In some cases, food truck owners hire a few more employees who are permanently based at the commissary kitchen or business office. Nonetheless, we can categorize staff into two groups:

• **Front of house:** Staff who interact with customers and handle customer-related duties, like taking orders, managing payments, responding to inquiries and feedback, and being brand ambassadors for your business.

• **Back of house:** Staff who handle all of the operational duties of the food truck, like picking up food ingredients, preparing and cooking food, cleaning, and bookkeeping.

The best employees for your food truck are those with diverse skills who can handle multiple tasks. Here is a list of roles your employees will need to manage:

• **Food truck window attendants:** Part of the front-of-house staff who take customer orders, issue order numbers, serve food and beverages, and accept payments. These employees must be professional and have exceptional communication and conflict resolution skills. They also must be knowledgeable about the menu, daily specials, and the food preparation process so that they can answer food-related questions customers may have.

• **Business manager:** A business or shift manager works in front and at the back of the house. Their job is to ensure that the business model, operational systems, and daily schedules are being followed and that inventory is always replenished. Depending on the size of your business, the manager can also handle the administrative and managerial duties of your food truck on your behalf while you set up and manage your other food trucks.

• **Chef and other cooks:** These people are part of the back-of-house crew who handle all of the food preparation and cooking. They are responsible for the kitchen operations—both in the truck and at the commissary kitchen. It's advised that the chef be involved in the hiring and management of junior chefs, since they will most likely train and manage junior chefs.

• **Kitchen workers:** If you have the budget for it, you can also hire kitchen workers. These employees aren't responsible for preparing or cooking the food but perform other kitchen tasks like peeling the vegetables, weighing ingredients, running to the store to buy more ingredients, or moving prepared food from the commissary kitchen to the food truck. To save costs on hiring separate cleaners, you can also make your kitchen workers responsible for cleaning and sanitizing the truck at the beginning and end of the workday.

• **Food truck drivers:** Depending on the size of your vehicle and the driving requirements in your city, you may need to hire a licensed truck driver to get your food truck from one location to the next. Alternatively, you can save on hiring costs and ensure that one of your permanent employees is a licensed truck driver.

THE QUALITIES OF AN EXCEPTIONAL EMPLOYEE

Seeking qualified employees who have the skills to perform their duties is one thing. You must also ensure that you hire people who you see yourself working with on a day-to-day basis. Along with the hard skills (qualifications and certifications), your employees need to have a few soft skills which are the interpersonal skills that help them work well with others. An exceptional employee is a hard worker but also a compassionate person, a student of life, and someone with an overall positive disposition. I could list so many qualities that describe an exceptional employee, but three are perhaps the most important: They are reliable, customer-oriented, and have a good knowledge of the industry.

Let's look at the first quality—reliability. A reliable person is consistent in how they perform and behave. This allows you to quickly build trust with them and show that they care about your business as much as you do. Reliable people can also be left to complete tasks on their own without missing deadlines or compromising on quality service delivery. If you are planning to leave your employees to manage your food truck during the day, you will need to trust that they will follow the business procedures and treat customers in a way that honors your brand. You will also need to trust that if you are not available for a few hours, they understand their duties and your expectations of them well enough to make decisions on the spot. Unfortunately, reliability is not something you can teach or can easily identify in someone when interviewing them, so you will need to monitor your employees and watch how consistent they are in working diligently.

The second quality is being customer-oriented. Being customer-oriented, or customer-centric, describes an employee who puts the customers' needs first. Every day at work, their mission is to help customers solve problems and achieve their goals. Customer-oriented employees will likely go above and beyond for customers without expecting compensation or any kind of acknowledgment in return. They do it because they genuinely value each customer and strive to create a community of loyal customers for the business. Customer-oriented employees also enjoy being around people and are usually empathetic. You can easily spot someone who isn't customer-oriented by how easily they become frustrated when faced with difficult customers. They don't have the patience or tolerance to allow customers to express themselves without getting offended.

Lastly, an exceptional employee has a good knowledge of the industry. Remember: The food truck industry looks and offers a different experience from the restaurant industry. If possible, you should consider hiring employees who have worked in food trucks before or any other mobile food businesses. Someone with experience in the food truck industry understands the importance of organizing lines of people, creating efficient ordering systems, preparing food in the quickest amount of time, and handling high order volumes. Since you are new to the food truck business, your experienced staff can help you put together your daily operational tasks and schedules based on models they have seen before. They can also offer you valuable insight into making your food truck business more profitable.

TIPS TO EMPLOY YOUR FIRST FOOD TRUCK EMPLOYEES

It's recommended to start looking for employees around three or four weeks before you open your food truck for business. When employing your first food truck crew, you can follow these tips:

Start by hiring your truck manager: Your truck manager will be the person responsible for overseeing all of the workers and operational procedures of your food truck business, so their role is the most important to fill. Ensure that their leadership style and personality match the kind of work environment you envision for your business.

Think carefully about the number of employees you need: While it may sound really good to have a crew of helpers, your start-up food truck business may not need so many helping hands. Consider the main tasks that you will need handled, like cooking, cleaning, and serving customers, and hire people who perform these duties (and similar smaller tasks).

Create job descriptions: Creating a job description not only helps you identify what kind of workers you need and the level of skill and experience they should have; it also helps prospective employees understand your expectations. Write a job summary, estimate of compensation, location of your food truck, estimate of hours they will be working, and driver's license requirements (if applicable). If you have any staff benefits, you can also highlight these on your description.

Advertise your job listings: Once you have an idea of how many employees you need and what you expect them to help you with, you can create a job listing online on recruitment platforms, or post your listing on Craigslist or on your social media pages. Your listing should include a brief summary of your company, the role candidates are applying for, and a summary of the job description and requirements. You can request candidates to fill out an online hiring form or email you for more details.

Set up interviews: Candidates who meet the job requirements will make it through to the interview stage. If you have a physical office, you can turn it into your interview venue; otherwise, you can also schedule interviews online. Remember to give candidates a realistic idea of what working for your food truck will entail and what they can look forward to.

When you have chosen your ideal employees, you will need to have an on-boarding strategy put in place, so they can get started immediately! Here are the legal steps to follow when hiring an employee for your food truck business:

1. Get an Employee Identification Number (EIN)

Before you hire an employee, you must obtain an EIN (or Employer Tax ID) from the U.S. Internal Revenue Services (IRS). This will help you report your taxes to the IRS. You can apply for an EIN online or visit your local IRS office.

2. Create Records for Withholding Taxes

The IRS expects businesses to keep records of employment taxes for at least four years. These records can also help you prepare financial statements and monitor your performance of the business. You need three types of withholding taxes for your business. The first one is the federal income tax withholding (a signed withholding exemption certificate that the business submits to the IRS on behalf of the employee). The second is a federal wage and tax statement that reports on the wages paid and taxes withheld for each employee. The last one is state taxes; depending on the state you live in, the IRS may require you to withhold state income taxes.

3. Ensure Your Employees Are Eligible to Work in the U.S.

According to federal law, business owners are required to verify their employees' eligibility to work in the U.S. After three days of working for the business, employers are required to complete the Form I-9 which is the employment eligibility verification form. You will need to examine your employee's citizenship status or work permit if they are a non-U.S. citizen. You are not required to submit this form to the federal government but instead to file them in your office and keep them for a maximum of three years or until the employee-employer contract has been terminated.

HOW TO MOTIVATE AND RETAIN YOUR EMPLOYEES

Like any other business in the food industry, employee turnover is high in the food truck business. It's common for employees to hop from one food business to another, leaving you understaffed. Where possible, it's good to put systems in place that encourage employees to remain loyal ambassadors of your business. Here are a few tips on motivating and retaining your employees:

Offer competitive wages: One of the best ways of ensuring your staff continues to work for you is to pay them competitive wages. Even though they may understand that you are running a small business and aren't making a lot of profits, your employees still have families to feed. If you cannot pay your workers as much as you would like to, offer them other benefits like a percentage increase in wages every year, or a 13th check at the end of the year.

Provide basic employee benefits: Another way to retain employees is to provide employee benefits, such as a retirement plan, medical aid, or insurance. Implementing this strategy not only helps you recruit some of the best jobseekers in the industry but also gives them a reason to work in your business for several years.

Consider other low-cost benefits: If you can't afford to offer basic employee benefits, think of alternative incentives you can offer your staff. These incentives should not substitute paying your employees fair wages, but instead, they should provide an added bonus. Some creative incentive suggestions include paying your employees weekly wages, giving them one free meal a day (or discounts on all meals), or offering them training opportunities.

Conduct quarterly performance reviews: Create performance objectives and review how your staff measure up to those objectives every few months. Schedule a meeting for each staff member where you reflect on their performance, offer feedback, and acknowledge significant achievement. Praise their strengths and offer support for their weaknesses. You can also reward outstanding performance reviews with a salary increase to motivate other staff members to meet performance objectives, too.

Create a work culture and drive it forward every day: Consider how you want your employees to feel when they come to work and write down a list of adjectives on a piece of paper. These adjectives will become the inspiration for the work culture you create. Hold yourself accountable to creating a work environment that supports the atmosphere you want your employees to work in. Key elements of an empowering work culture include encouraging open communication, offering educational or career advancement opportunities, and rewarding outstanding work.

CHAPTER 11
IT'S OPENING DAY!

N othing could've prepared me for the launch of my food truck. I had spent many long nights planning what time I would arrive, how I would greet customers, and the signature dishes I would prepare on that day. I traveled across the city looking for chef's uniforms—so myself and two other employees would look sharp and professional in the kitchen—made a stop at my suppliers to pick up my fresh produce, and made sure my kitchen equipment was plugged in and ready to grill some food!

But in all of the planning and preparation I had done, I forgot one crucial component: creating a digital marketing strategy that would launch my business online. Oops! I guess that was my $1,000 mistake. While my physical launch was successful, and I managed to feed 50 hungry customers, I regretted not establishing my online presence in time, so I could reach more customers and receive more sales. After my launch, while I was cleaning up, I decided to take a photo of my food truck and post it online, captioning it: "Successful first day."

Within 10 minutes, I had received over 100 likes, and people were asking me where my truck was based and what kinds of foods I sold. I couldn't believe it! Just as I thought I had missed a marketing opportunity of a lifetime, I was able to bounce back and engage with potential customers online! From that day onward, I promised myself that I would prioritize my digital marketing as much as the daily promotions I offered customers on the truck. Within six months, we had 10,000 followers, and the numbers are still pouring in even today.

Congratulations for making it this far into the book. Absorbing all of the information written here isn't an easy feat, but you managed to do it! Now that you're near completing this book, I would like to give you some advice on making your launch day memorable. While it's good to consider factors like what food you will prepare or which location you will park first, you should remember to document your journey online so that you can appeal to a wider audience of potential customers who may be enthusiastic about supporting your business. In this chapter, we will discuss marketing strategies that you can implement on your opening day, so it can receive the kind of traction you desire.

BEFORE THE OPENING DAY

About a few weeks before you launch your food truck, create your launch day digital marketing strategy. This will include all of the marketing tactics you wish to implement on the first day of business. Your digital marketing strategy will promote creative content to people who fall under your target market and entice them to visit your food truck at some point during the day or week. A great digital marketing strategy includes several channels, like your business website, blog, and social media channels, which you use to reach members of your target market online. When planning your marketing tactics, consider your various channels and how you can use them to propel your business to greater heights.

Here are a few marketing tactics to consider when planning a digital marketing strategy:

1. Show Photos of Menu Items

On your first day, no one knows who you are or what your business is about. It's up to you to market your product offerings by showing potential customers the kinds of dishes you prepare in your truck. Sharing photos is one of the best ways to sell food, since people eat with their eyes first. You can tantalize their taste buds by capturing high-quality photos of your foods and posting them on your social media pages or website on your launch day. In the captions, describe the name of the dish and a summary of ingredients. If your dishes cater to people with specific dietary requirements, include that information in the caption, too.

2. Use QR Codes

You can direct the foot traffic you receive on launch day to your social media pages by using QR codes. When a customer scans a QR code with their smartphone, they are directed to any one of your digital channels. It could be one of your social media pages or maybe your website. This can be a great way of encouraging first-time buyers to join your online community and stay up to date with special offers you may carry out. Using QR codes also removes the need of having traditional business cards or pamphlets which have become ineffective marketing tools over the years.

3. Take up Space on Social Media

It's not enough to participate on one social media platform when your customers are spread across multiple platforms. You will need to study the social media usage behaviors of your target market and create a page on every platform they use. Younger consumers are typically on every social media platform but tend to spend more time on video-sharing platforms like YouTube or TikTok. If you are appealing to a younger market, you would need to have an account on these platforms and find creative ways of sharing content. You can also use different platforms for different marketing objectives. For example, Facebook is great for brand awareness and education, while Twitter is great for broadcasting announcements and sharing discount codes.

4. Create an Online-Only Discount Deal

Another great way to create an online buzz is to offer online-only discounts. Customers have the opportunity to save money on their meals by making preorders and paying online. Not only does this ensure that you meet your order target, but it can also offer customers an alternative method of placing orders and paying for them. Avoid implementing this strategy regularly, as customers might get used to paying discounted rates instead of paying the full cost of meals. Only use it when you desire to boost sales; during special holidays or events; or when you are promoting a new dish on your menu.

5. Engage With Your Customers

Customers want to feel like they are a part of your growing community. You can make them feel welcome by engaging with them frequently online. Make it a habit to respond in your brand's tone and language. Remember that even though you are building long-lasting friendships, you are still communicating with customers; therefore, a level of professionalism is required. Dedicate special times during the day when you respond to comments and private messages. Be polite when dealing with emotional customers, and always seek to go above and beyond in meeting their needs. You can also post great customer reviews that you have received online and encourage customers to tag you in photos where your food is featured. When you notice your engagement is dropping, find creative ways of appealing to your followers, like creating a competition, starting a challenge, or running a poll.

CHECKLIST FOR MAKING MEGA SALES ON YOUR FIRST DAY

I know, I know: You want to make thousands of dollars on your first day. You have already invested so much money into building your food truck business, and all you want is to see long lines of customers waiting patiently for their turn to buy food from your truck. This is the ultimate food truck dream, but it can certainly become your reality! I have seen many food trucks sell out on their produce on their first day with many customers buying multiple items for them and their friends to sample. Your food truck can achieve this level of success on its first day, too, but to do so, you will need to invest in your marketing. There are five main components you will need to check off your list before launch day to ensure that your business is geared to succeed. These include:

1. Branding

If you opened your food truck 5–10 years ago, you probably wouldn't have as much competition as you will now. The only way to differentiate your business from other food truck businesses is to focus on creating a distinct brand. Your brand is made up of several elements, such as your brand name, logo, objectives, beliefs, personality, colors, and so on. Even though your brand includes many elements, they should all relate with one another so that your brand carries a clear, consistent, and powerful message. Having elements that clash may lead to doubts about what you truly stand for. For example, if you build a brand around supporting veganism, your logo shouldn't make any references to meat (like having a huge image of a juicy burger). Moreover, ensure consistency by using the same fonts, colors, and language on every marketing platform.

2. Website

Since consumers use the Internet as a tool to search for their favorite businesses, you should create a website that introduces your business in a way that is true to your brand. Your website can also become a great way to build trust with your prospective customers. You can post copies of your permits and health clearances, show them the inside of your truck, allow them to view your menu, and even include a video clip where you introduce the rest of your team.

3. Social Media Marketing

We have already spoken about the importance of marketing your business online, especially on your social media platforms. However, we haven't discussed some promotional ideas that you can use on social media. Here are a few to consider:

Giveaways: If you want to build a social media following in the shortest amount of time, you can host giveaways where you give away free promotional items (like your business merchandise) or vouchers for free meals at your food truck. Make sure that you give out clear instructions on how to participate as well as certain terms and conditions that may apply.

Contests: These work in a similar way to giveaways, although the prize does not have to include free product items (just make them enticing enough for followers to participate). Provide clear contest entry details, and mention when the contest closes. Make a big spectacle when you announce the winners and capture the moment on camera, so you can post it up on your social media.

Word-of-mouth marketing: The quickest way to get business referrals is through word-of-mouth marketing. People who have never heard of your business are more likely to visit your truck after being referred to you by a friend. You can leverage word-of-mouth marketing by creating a referral system where customers share specific discount codes with their friends and family to use at your food truck. With each successful referral, they themselves get discounts on meals, too!

You can also choose to carry out different promotions on each social media platform. Here are some examples:

Facebook: This is ideal when you want to share business information, respond to customer questions, and post about your upcoming events.

Twitter: Tweets are useful when keeping customers up to date on your whereabouts, like sharing a live tweet on your location. You can also use your Twitter page to share emergency announcements—for instance, if there are certain dishes that have sold out. If your brand supports a societal cause, you can tweet statements that show your customers where you stand on the matter.

Instagram: This is great for sharing images and videos of your food and cooking processes. Your customers may want to see pictures of you selecting produce, preparing food, or engaging with customers. Influencer marketing works well on platforms like Instagram where popular foodies, chefs, or celebrities are seen standing at your food truck or taking a bite of your food.

TikTok: Great for video-based short clips that show elements of your business. For example, you can make a TikTok video showing your chef preparing a meal, a compilation of positive reviews from customers, any food challenges that you create, or recordings of your surroundings (like filming the atmosphere at a festival or a farmer's market).

4. Food Truck Apps

There are a few food truck apps created by tech developers that help over 25,000 food truck businesses in the U.S. market their food trucks. Advertising your food truck through an app ensures that you connect with your ideal target market rather than cross your fingers that you will find them online. Here are two popular food truck apps that you can join:

"WTF!?! Where's The Foodtruck?" Vendor App: This app helps food truck businesses share their location across major U.S. cities, promotes their product offerings, and facilitates in-app ordering. It also promotes social media and website links and connects food truck businesses to catering and events opportunities.

Roaming Hunger: The most popular food truck app used in America, Europe, and China. It allows food truck businesses to create accounts, share their live locations, and promote their special discounts and offers to hungry Roaming Hunger users. Like WTF, it also connects food truck businesses to catering and event opportunities.

5. Merchandising

When you have established a strong customer base, selling merchandise can encourage your loyal customers to become brand ambassadors. In order for your merchandise to sell, it should match your typical customer's sense of style and look like a piece of clothing or accessory they would wear out in public. You should also make sure that your merchandise relates to an element of your brand. For example, if you are selling baked goods, you can sell custom oven mitts. Here is a list of common merchandising items that customers love:

- T-shirts
- Stickers
- Travel mugs
- Caps
- Keychains
- Bracelets

These items may seem cliché, but customers love them because they can easily merge into their daily lives. For example, a customer who buys coffee from your stand every morning will use your branded coffee mug at home.

CHAPTER 12
THE WAY TO YOUR CUSTOMERS' HEARTS

After the launch, your number-one priority as a food truck owner will be to make your business sustainable. How do you do this? Well, it's simple. You will need to concentrate on building and promoting your brand. Think about where you would like to see your business in the next 5–10 years. I bet you have ambitions of buying more trucks and setting up several food truck businesses across your city or in other parts of the U.S. Like any franchise business, you will need to have a powerful brand that is recognized and loved by many customers in order for it to succeed. In this final chapter, I will discuss strategies for building a strong brand and give you tips on making your business sustainable through the years.

FOOD TRUCK BRANDING 101

There are new businesses that launch online every day. Each business competes with the next to get the consumers' attention. It's becoming harder for businesses that don't have brands to remain competitive, since customers are more likely to relate to content that appeals to their interests, communicates a strong message, and leaves them with many burning questions. Think of a brand as the face mask businesses wear that allows them to connect and engage with members of their target market. Through the brand, a business is able to build a relationship with potential customers and eventually turn them into loyal supporters.

A powerful brand has a specific persona, or identity, that looks and feels like a real person. In fact, when a customer engages with a good brand, they forget that they are actually supporting a business rather than a good friend. Whenever people speak about brands, they are quick to mention brand elements like fonts, logos, and colors. While these elements make up a brand, they don't explain the essence of a brand. The real essence of a brand is in establishing a long-lasting bond with a customer. This is done through building trust, sharing milestones, going above and beyond for customers, predicting customer needs, and finding ways to give back to your community.

In other words, if you want to build a strong brand, you will need to develop friendships with your customers through each content piece you post and every meal you serve. There are also two additional factors that can strengthen the relationships you develop with your customers and, in doing so, strengthen your brand. These two factors are creating memorable experiences and forming emotional connections.

Reflect back on a positive memory where you were with your close friends or family. Think back to what you were doing and how you felt at the time. You will notice that the details of the event aren't as strong as the emotions that you still capture in your heart. This is the same when customers visit your food truck and order meals or engage with you online. They may not remember the details of your interactions with them, but they will remember how you made them feel. Having a strong brand is about capturing the hearts of your customers in everything you do. Once you have captured their hearts, your brand is recorded in their brains and labeled as a positive memory. Each time they drive past your truck or scroll past your content on social media, they will feel obliged to show their support.

Now that you know the essence of a powerful brand, here are a few points about what a powerful brand looks like:

A powerful brand is easy to recognize: Its mission and objectives are simple and captivating. It focuses on emphasizing a few elements—not all of them. It has unique symbols that make it easy for you to recall it in future.

A powerful brand has a strong emotional appeal: It connects to a deep desire that a customer has and makes their desire come true. It knows how to listen to its customers and intuitively sense what they need. It is responsive and gives off positive energy.

A powerful brand is consistent: Whether the brand is marketing to people on the ground or to an online audience, its messages are consistent on all channels. It sounds the same whether the business is performing well or not. When it makes a promise, it honors it, and customers know exactly what to excerpt from it.

A powerful brand offers a unique experience: It takes the customer on a journey and exposes them to new interests and adventures. Customers feel richer, happier, healthier, or more cultured after spending time with a powerful brand.

If you have design skills, you can create your own logo and graphics on free graphic design software like Canva. Alternatively, you can seek help from a graphic designer who can create a visual identity for your brand. Working with a graphic designer may come at a cost, but it will ensure that your brand elements are consistent with each other, and your brand looks professional on all platforms.

HOW TO MAINTAIN FOOD TRUCK CUSTOMERS

As good as it feels having a customer purchase a meal from your truck, it feels even better when you see the same customer visiting time and time again. The longevity of your business relies on repeat customers who find reasons to visit your truck on a regular basis. Here are a few tips on how you can keep customers coming back for more of your food:

Create a memorable concept: When coming up with your food truck concept, think out of the box and create a brand that appeals to a certain market's needs and desires. Don't worry about being misunderstood by everyone else. As long as the people you are serving can connect to you, your business will make sales.

Integrate technology in your business model: Your customers use technology in many aspects of their lives, so you should adopt savvy technological tools to offer your customers greater convenience. An example of this would be offering mobile ordering and payment solutions.

Switch up your menu seasonally: Give loyal customers something to look forward to by adding new products to the menu each season. Prepare these new dishes using seasonal ingredients so that you don't spend a lot of money producing new meals.

Partner with other local businesses: Find other food truck businesses selling non-competitive foods and find ways to support each other and make profits together. You can also look at partnering with corporations and offering catering services at a discounted rate or partnering with wedding planners and other event coordinators and sharing profits from each event.

Offer delivery services: To succeed in the long run, you will need to think about serving customers who don't have time to stand in a line for food. Having a preordering and delivery system can make it easier for customers to pay and get their food delivered to them without having to leave their homes or offices. To offer delivery services, you can partner with third-party delivery websites like Grubhub or Eat24Hours. Alternatively, if you have a driver, you can have them deliver food to customers within a certain mile radius.

CHAPTER 13
CONCLUSION

You have made it this far, and I'd like to know this from you: How was the journey? Did your ideas of what a food truck business entails change during the course of reading this book? Even though I have shared with you the beginner's guide to starting your own food truck business, I guarantee you that there are still some lessons you will only learn once you get your business off the ground.

As much freedom and creative expression as a food truck business offers you, remember that at the end of the day, it is still a business and will most likely come with the daily struggles many entrepreneurs face. However, the kinds of struggles you will encounter running your food truck are different from the many stressful challenges faced by restaurant owners. The advantage with your business model is that it requires less start-up capital which means that even if you don't perform well during the first few months, you won't incur as many financial losses.

My first food truck failed, but that was because I went in thinking I didn't need to invest time in doing research and compiling my business plan. I thought that watching a few YouTube videos would provide me with the necessary training to manage my finances, employees, and sustain my business in the long term. It turns out I was wrong, but that didn't deter me. I went back to the drawing board, and this time, it took me a few months to do careful planning. The difference in how I ran my first food truck to how I ran the second one was like night and day!

I understand that all of this information may be a lot for you to take in right now. That's why you should treat this book like a manual and focus on each individual chapter until you feel you have mastered it and ticked off every checkbox that you need to. Reminding yourself about all of the minor and major details you need to consider will give you the confidence you need to build a strong foundation for your food truck business.

Before I end off the book, I will leave you with a few cautionary reminders that will summarize many of the lessons you have learned along this journey:

1. Don't Choose the Wrong Product

A wrong product is one that doesn't have a high demand, is too expensive to produce, and doesn't appeal to your target market. Do your market research and calculate the variable costs associated with producing each dish before you decide to put it on your menu.

2. Don't Choose the Wrong Truck

A wrong truck is one that is not within your budget range; is either too big or too small; and requires too much maintenance work. While it's advised for start-up food trucks to go for used vehicles, make sure that you do your vehicle inspections and select a used car that is in good condition.

3. Don't Forget to Invest in Your Marketing

Your food truck is a moving billboard that attracts the eyes of many pedestrians in the city. Customizing your truck in a visually appealing way will help you market your business without even trying. However, there are many customers who don't live in your location or visit the streets where you park. These customers can be found online. Take as much time in creating an online community as you do in creating mouthwatering menus. Capture your customers' hearts by engaging with them online and creating memorable experiences each time they place an order.

4. Don't Bite Off More Than You Can Chew

As a start-up entrepreneur, you should always find ways to save money rather than splurge on items that won't necessarily bring a return. Create a reasonable budget and stick to it. If you cannot afford kitchen equipment, consider leasing them until you can comfortably afford owning brand new ones. If it costs too much to attend a festival, consider skipping it and saving up to attend the next one.

5. **Don't Quit When It Gets Rough**

Do you know what entrepreneurs don't tell you about owning a business? It can sometimes be extremely stressful. Business owners are constantly thinking about different aspects of their business and looking for solutions to big problems. When you catch yourself feeling anxious, take a deep breath, and remind yourself that you are running a marathon—not a sprint. You need to pace yourself and invest enough time in acquiring funds to start your business, grow your customer base, and build a sustainable brand. These milestones cannot be reached overnight or even in a year. Be patient with yourself and focus on mastering the work that you do.

There you have it—a comprehensive beginner's book on how to start your food truck business from scratch. All that's left for you to do now is to begin compiling your business plan. (Refer to Chapter 2 when you get stuck.) Remember: Slow and steady wins the race. The journey of building your food truck empire starts now!

If you have found this book valuable, please consider leaving a review. We thank you for your feedback.

CHAPTER 14
REFERENCES

Business Plan Template. (2021, July 1). *Food truck business plan template*. Business Plan Template. https://www.businessplantemplate.com/food-truck-business-plan-template/

CardConnect. (n.d.). *Food truck startup costs*. CardConnect. https://cardconnect.com/launchpointe/running-a-business/food-truck-startup-costs

Cynthia, E. (2020, February 19). *10 Strategies to get the best pricing for a food truck menu*. Profitable Venture. https://www.profitableventure.com/food-truck-menu-pricing-strategies/

Editorial Team. (2019, May 2). *How top food trucks pick the best spots*. Clover Blog. https://blog.clover.com/how-top-food-trucks-pick-the-best-spots/

Elkins, K. (2019, September 20). *Opening a food truck costs about $100,000—here are all of the expenses that come with running one.* CNBC. https://www.cnbc.com/2019/09/20/the-hidden-costs-of-running-a-food-truck.html

Entrepreneur Staff. (2015, May 11). *Food trucks 101: Where to stock up on ingredients.* Entrepreneur. https://www.entrepreneur.com/article/233383

Fairfax County. (n.d.). *Health permits for mobile food service units.* Fairfax County. https://www.fairfaxcounty.gov/health/permits/mobile-food-unit

Ferdman, R. (2011, April). *A day in the life of a food truck.* Cooking Channel. https://www.cookingchanneltv.com/devour/2011/04/a-day-in-the-life-of-a-food-truck

FoodTruckr. (2013, November 20). *Food truck branding 101: Build a brand that rocks.* FoodTruckr. https://foodtruckr.com/marketing/food-truck-branding-101-build-brand-rocks/

FoodTruckr. (2017, January 10). *3 Tips for hiring your first employee at your food truck business.* FoodTruckr. https://foodtruckr.com/business/tips-for-hiring-your-first-employee-at-your-food-truck-business/

FoodTruckr. (2020, May 28). *How to start a food truck 19: Organize your licenses and permits.* FoodTruckr. https://foodtruckr.com/business/start-food-truck-19-organize-licenses-permits/

ForbesQuotes. (n.d.). *Thoughts On The Business Of Life.* Forbes. https://www.forbes.com/quotes/5037/

Gud Capital. (n.d.). *Food truck loans: Financing options for food truck businesses.* Gud Capital. https://gudcapital.com/food-truck-loans/

Hangover Staff. (2019). *Coca-Cola prices [Updated 2019].* Hangover Prices. https://www.hangoverprices.com/coca-cola-prices/

Howmuchisit Staff. (2018, August 9). *How Much Do French Fries Cost? | HowMuchIsIt.org.* How Much Is It. https://www.howmuchisit.org/how-much-do-french-fries-cost/#:~:text=On%20average%2C%20French%20fries%20at

IbisWorld. (2021, July 30). *Food trucks in the US - Market size 2005–2027.* IbisWorld. https://www.ibisworld.com/industry-statistics/market-size/food-trucks-united-states/#:~:text=The%20market%20size%2C%20measured%20by

Karpatia Trucks. (2020). *How to choose the perfect food truck size.* Karpatia Trucks. https://karpatiatrucks.com/food-truck-size-and-dimensions/

Krook, D. (2019, October 1). *Licenses you need to run a food truck.* Touch Bistro. https://www.touchbistro.com/blog/licenses-you-need-to-run-a-food-truck/

Lee, W. K. (2019, November 9). *Top 5 most profitable food and beverage business ideas you should start.* Wilson K Lee.

https://wilsonklee.com/blog/top-5-most-profitable-food-beverage-business-ideas/

Lightspeed. (2021, March 23). *The ultimate guide to creating the perfect food truck menu concept.* Lightspeed. https://www.lightspeedhq.co.uk/blog/food-truck-menu-concepts/

M&R. (2018, April 9). *Five popular food truck alternatives to start a mobile food business.* MR Trailers. https://www.mr-trailers.com/food-truck-alternatives/

Marticio, D. (2021, April 21). *Food truck financing: The best food truck loans for 2021.* Value Penguin. https://www.valuepenguin.com/small-business/best-food-truck-loans

Miles, S. (2018, June 29). *How food trucks can leverage location data to optimize sales.* Street Fight Magazine. https://streetfightmag.com/2018/06/29/how-food-trucks-can-leverage-location-data-to-optimize-sales/

Morgaine, B. (2017, May 12). *9 Strategies to increase your food truck revenue.* Bplans Blog. https://articles.bplans.com/10-strategies-to-increase-your-food-truck-revenue/

Myrick, R. (n.d.-a). *Determine your food truck's staffing needs.* Dummies. https://www.dummies.com/business/start-a-business/determine-your-food-trucks-staffing-needs/

Myrick, R. (n.d.-b). *How to motivate and retain your food truck staff.* Dummies. https://www.dummies.com/business/

start-a-business/how-to-motivate-and-retain-your-food-truck-staff/

Myrick, R. (2017, July 12). *Sourcing local food for your food truck menu ingredients.* Mobile Cuisine. https://mobile-cuisine.com/menu-design/sourcing-local-food-food-truck-menu/

Myrick, R. (2018, January 9). *Avoid these food truck menu pricing strategies.* Mobile Cuisine. https://mobile-cuisine.com/menu-design/avoid-food-truck-menu-pricing-strategies/

Myrick, R. (2020, May 1). *Food truck employees: How to employ your first.* Mobile Cuisine. https://mobile-cuisine.com/human-resources/food-truck-employees/

Nightingale, J. (2021, April 28). *What to look for before you buy a used food truck.* Restaurant Engine. https://restaurantengine.com/what-to-look-for-before-you-buy-a-used-food-truck/

O'Chucks, S. (2017, August 25). *Should you rent or buy a used food truck? (cost comparison).* Profitable Venture. https://www.profitableventure.com/buy-rent-food-truck-cost/

Oden, G. (2018, May 11). *How to start a food truck business: A cost breakdown.* Innovative Ideas & Solutions. https://posbistro.com/blog/how-to-start-food-truck-cost-breakdown/

Perkins, R. (2019, October 28). *Food truck marketing: 10 Ways to improve your social media strategy.* Custom Concessions. https://www.customconcessionsusa.com/food-truck-marketing-10-ways-to-improve-your-social-media-strategy/

Poirier-Leroy, O. (2019, July 16). *How Michael Phelps used visualization to stay calm under pressure.* Your Swim Log. https://www.yourswimlog.com/michael-phelps-visualization/

Priceonomics. (2017, April 7). *How much do the ingredients cost in your favorite foods?* Forbes. https://www.forbes.com/sites/priceonomics/2017/04/07/how-much-do-the-ingredients-cost-in-your-favorite-foods/?sh=70b855d411ed

Sage. (2019). *How much does it cost to open a restaurant checklist.* Sage. https://www.sage.com/en-us/accounting-software/startup-costs/restaurant/

Seppala, E. (2020, February 20). *How to start and fund a food truck business.* Merchant Maverick. https://www.merchantmaverick.com/start-food-truck-business/

Sheetz, D. (2020, November 3). *Food trucks and food safety-A look into mobile hygiene.* Ziphaccp. https://ziphaccp.com/en/food-safety/food-truck-food-safety.html

Staff. (2019, December 18). *How to write a food truck business plan.* Food Truck Empire. https://foodtruckempire.com/podcast/business-plan/

Support Staff. (2013, June 13). *Food trucks: Should you rent or buy?* Food Truck Empire. https://foodtruckempire.com/interviews/rent-or-buy/

Support Staff. (2019, May 16). *The best 8 food truck menu ideas: #6 Costs less than $5 to make.* Food Truck Empire. https://foodtruckempire.com/how-to/food-truck-menu-ideas/

Sweeney, D. (2019, June 18). *4 Licenses and permits food trucks need to operate.* Score. https://www.score.org/blog/4-licenses-and-permits-food-trucks-need-operate

The Restaurant Times. (2016, November 21). *5 Reasons why you should open a food truck instead of a regular restaurant.* The Restaurant Times. https://www.posist.com/restaurant-times/restro-gyaan/5-reasons-why-you-should-open-a-food-truck-instead-of-a-regular-restaurant.html

Traylor, R. (2020, March 16). *Deep dive: Does your food truck operation need a commissary kitchen?* Food Truck Operator. https://www.foodtruckoperator.com/blogs/deep-dive-does-your-food-truck-operation-need-a-commissary-kitchen/

Webstaurant Store. (2021a, June 15). *Food truck marketing.* WebstaurantStore. https://www.webstaurantstore.com/article/146/food-truck-marketing.html

Webstaurant Store. (2021b, September 7). *Food truck equipment checklist.* Webstaurant Store. https://www.webstaurantstore.com/article/398/food-truck-equipment-list.html

Wong, B. (2015, February 6). *7 Challenges food truck owners must overcome.* Bindolabs. https://bindolabs.com/blog/7-challenges-food-truck-owners-must-overcome

Zac's Burgers. (2017, August 1). *10 Tips for creating your food truck menu board.* Zac's Burgers. https://zacsburgers.com/10-tips-creating-food-truck-menu-board/

Thank you for choosing this book. If you have enjoyed this book or found it to be helpful, please consider leaving a review on Amazon.

To go directly to the review page, you can:

- Scan the QR-code below with the camera on your phone
- Or type in the Shorturl link above the QR-code in your internet browser

shorturl.at/HMEIK

Made in the USA
Las Vegas, NV
16 November 2022